Walking Tall

Key steps to total image impact

Walking Tall

Key steps to total image impact

Lesley Everett

THE McGRAW-HILL COMPANIES

London · Burr Ridge IL · New York · St Louis · San Francisco
Auckland · Bogotá · Caracas · Lisbon · Madrid · Mexico · Milan
Montreal · New Delhi · Panama · Paris · San Juan · São Paulo
Singapore · Sydney · Tokyo · Toronto

The McGraw·Hill Companies

WALKING TALL: KEY STEPS TO TOTAL IMAGE IMPACT
Lesley Everett
0077099672

Published by McGraw-Hill Professional
Shoppenhangers Road
Maidenhead
Berkshire
SL6 2QL
Telephone: 44 (0) 1628 502 500
Fax: 44 (0) 1628 770 224
Website: www.mcgraw-hill.co.uk

British Library Cataloguing in Publication Data
A catalogue record for this book is available from the British Library
Library of Congress Cataloguing in Publication Data
The Library of Congress data for this book
has been applied for/is available from the Library of Congress

Sponsoring Editor: Elizabeth Robinson
Editorial Assistant: Sarah Butler
Business Marketing Manager: Elizabeth McKeever
Production Editorial Manager: Max Elvey
Desk Editor: Eleanor Hayes

Text design by Claire Brodmann
Typeset by RefineCatch Limited, Bungay, Suffolk
Printed and bound by Clays Ltd, Bungay, Suffolk
Cover design by Senate Design Ltd

McGraw-Hill books are available at special quantity discounts. Please contact the Corporate
Sales Executive at the above address.

Contents

Acknowledgements

Twenty years ago, when I struggled with A-level English essays, I would never have dreamed that this book would be possible. It is with thanks to many people that *Walking Tall* has materialized, because it has been written from a whole bunch of experience gained throughout my life and business career so far. For that experience I'd like to thank all the inspiring people I've worked with over the past 20 years and especially my valued clients.

Huge thanks to the special man in my life, my husband David, who has continually believed in me and given me superhuman support during the tough bits.

To my Mum and Dad, who never fail to make me feel proud of what I do and who help to make my achievements so meaningful for me.

To Sue Blake, my dedicated agent and PR, who gave me the initial encouragement to write the book. Sue, you're a star and an absolute rock – thank you.

I want to thank my publishers, who gave me the opportunity to create this book. Thanks for putting up with my fussiness and for being so patient. I'm sure it's been an experience.

To all my loyal friends (you know who you are), who have tirelessly listened, offered advice and been a sounding board for my thoughts and ideas. My social life will be back to normal shortly – promise!

And lastly, I'd like to dedicate this book, my first but not my last, to my wonderful son, Max. If ever there were a budding image consultant in the making, it's you. You're the only nine-year-old that I take tips from about my image! Long may it continue sweetheart.

My love and *sincere* thanks to you all for your unique and individual inspiration.

Lesley Everett

What Key Business People Say About Image

In each of its businesses, Virgin undertakes quite a comprehensive range of different training and personal development programmes, depending in scope on the individual business. Almost all Virgin businesses are people businesses, therefore image training is one of our top priorities.

Sir Richard Branson – *Chairman, Virgin Group of Companies*

Because fashions have changed, and in many cases business dress has become less formal, there is a temptation to believe that personal appearance is less important. In practice, nothing could be further from the truth. Appearance matters as much as ever: perhaps more so in an age where there is less uniformity. Like it or not, the way we look has a major impact on the impression we make and the influence we exert.

George Cox – *Director-General of the Institute of Directors*

First impressions are critical for success. The message is simple . . . if you want career success it is essential that you invest some time in ensuring that your personal image is at its very best.

Jo Bond – *Managing Director, Right Management Consultants UK*

Organizations are a reflection of the leadership in terms of their language, behaviour, attitudes and, of course, image.

Sue Cheshire – *Managing Director, The Academy for Chief Executives*

Having all the right competencies, achievements and skills is not enough in the 21st century to get on in our careers. We all must develop the skill of creating and maintaining a positive impression, and a key integral part of that is getting our packaging right.

Hilary Wilson – *Leading Career Strategist*

Introduction
Why all the Fuss?

WHY ALL THE FUSS ABOUT PERSONAL image? Because research consistently shows that first impressions are based on what we *see*, rather than what we *hear*. No matter how hard we try to be unbiased or uninfluenced by somebody's appearance, studies convincingly prove that first and lasting impressions are significantly shaped by the visual image we are presented with. Our 'personal branding' is a persuasive tool each and every one of us has at our disposal to use to maximize a positive image impact in business. However, the *power* of our personal brand is often overlooked and, as such, it is either not used to its maximum potential or, worse still, it can get in the way of projecting our true qualities and abilities. If you form a bad or even poor initial impression of somebody, do you really change your mind when somebody else tells you positive things about him or her? At best we give that person a second chance, but we're still influenced by our initial impression. In recent studies in support of *Walking Tall* we found that 80 per cent of business professionals we spoke to agree that they form impressions on how well a colleague may do his or her job by their clothing and grooming. It would seem conclusive, then, that, whether we like it or not, we will be judged and will continue to be judged on visual first impressions.

In areas such as sales, and client-facing and customer-service environments, a positive personal brand is more obviously a vital ingredient for business success. However, the visual messages from the chief executive to the receptionist must be synonymous with the corporate identity reflected by all selling mechanisms in the organization – the corporate branding, marketing, advertising and logos. Presenting the desired message cohesively through all these media, in particular the people, adds up to business success. People, however, are often missed out of the corporate branding strategy. In my experience as a personal branding expert in the UK, I am now working with more and more companies in commerce and industry to deliver personal image training. It is now apparent to me that more organizations than ever are tuning into the strongest brand message and differentiator they have – their people. Is yours? In response to questions I put to Richard Branson, he told me that:

> *Virgin has always worked on the general philosophy of staff first, customers second and shareholders third. This may sound the wrong way round but we've always believed that if we look after our people well they will look after our customers better and as a result shareholders will benefit in the long term. It seems to have worked so far!*

Forward-thinking professionals now regard CPD (Continuing Professional Development) as sacrosanct to their career progression, and personal brand development is a key element of this initiative.

In a business climate now operating around the clock, across a global network through the Internet and video conferencing, traditional face-to-face communication is apparently becoming less important. In my world it isn't. Many of my clients recognize that the fast-paced business world we work in relies *even more* on traditional qualities – quality people portraying a quality image in a quality organization. Today, time is always limited and we have to make instantaneous decisions often; therefore, we use our intuition and, most importantly, the visual first impression to make that decision.

One of the greatest business misnomers in modern times was the introduction of Dress-down Friday. Starting in the United States and sweeping across Europe, many businessmen and women here in the UK have been at a loss as to how to do the dress-down 'thing' *and* still retain their credibility and professionalism. Without adequate guidelines smart/casual has been open to misinterpretation and many companies are now reverting 'back to suits'. Because dress-down has been instrumental in creating an inconsistent corporate message, a whole chapter is dedicated to it in *Walking Tall*.

Walking Tall is an authoritative book on how to create a positive image impact in business, for anyone currently in business, or returning to it, at any level, at any time. Personal branding skills you will learn from reading *Walking Tall* will help you to succeed at interviews, increase your earnings potential, ascend the career ladder quicker, increase business performance and achieve the look of quality appropriate for every business situation. Be prepared to 'think outside the boxes' when it comes to developing your personal brand – *Walking Tall* is an empowering book devoted to helping you to maximize your personal potential.

Whatever your career, lifestyle, specific objectives and goals, I hope that *Walking Tall* helps you to achieve image confidence, recognition and fabulous exposure to brilliant opportunities during your career. Send me an email to *walkingtall@leconsultants.co.uk* if there are specific or individual queries you would like answered.

Be happy, keep smiling and Walk Tall – and do let me know about your personal successes from reading the book.

chapter 1

Personifying the Corporate Brand

A New Dimension

CORPORATE BRANDING, A TERM TALKED about a great deal in today's competitive business world, is essential to the success of any organization, whether it is a multi-national or a smaller, privately owned company. The world is a much more competitive place than it was even five years ago, and businesses are having to focus even more on their brand values if they are to retain their customer base, let alone attract new customers. However, one factor is constantly overlooked in achieving and reinforcing corporate branding – the people.

In this chapter I want to introduce the *human* element of branding – that is, how you, as individuals, create an added and vital dimension to corporate identity. Because you've picked up this book, you obviously already have an interest in improving and increasing your *personal* impact, and by consciously reflecting the corporate brand, you, by the very nature of that awareness, will be maximizing your opportunities for greater exposure, promotion and ultimately success. There has to be a correlation between a company's image and the image presented by its staff for corporate messages to be heard, believed and accepted.

Consistency is Key

Not only is a brand essential if a company hopes to maximize its sales of products and services, but it must be projected consistently. A consistency must be developed that customers understand and are drawn to. On asking delegates in my seminars to define the elements that are integral to corporate identity, they will generally come up with the obvious areas such as logos, advertising, website, marketing collateral, office premises, packaging and sometimes uniforms. All of these combine to create the corporate identity, and they all reflect the brand. However, many organizations will stop short of maximizing their vast investment in corporate branding by not ensuring that their staff, the biggest asset that any company has, also reflect those same brand values.

Corporate branding should be targeted at the company's people too, not just at the outside world. As Wally Olins says in his book *Corporate Identity*, 'If the staff convey the values – how they look and act – and pass that on to customers, then the company succeeds'. After all, we know that people buy from *people*, so this should be a major consideration when investing in a corporate brand, but all too often companies fail to train their staff in the projection of this image. This is starting to improve as companies realize that image is integral to their organization, and to their ultimate success. Any branding expert will tell you that the main element of branding is consistency. Without consistency you don't have a brand. Therefore, no organization can have a totally successful brand if its staff are not reflecting those values all of the time. Companies such as TXU Energi that advocate that they 'like to go the extra mile' will be in danger of losing all credibility if they don't do just that, and if McDonald's, Coca-Cola, Disney and BMW didn't deliver according to their brand messages, they wouldn't be the global successes they are – understood, bought and valued by us. The success of a brand can be seriously damaged in a flash if one employee, be it the receptionist or senior management, displays unprofessional behaviour. The perception is, 'if the company employs people who are unprofessional and can't communicate effectively, what other sloppy standards does it harbour in its midst and what sort of service can I expect to receive?' Consider this, as Andrew Smith, the chief executive officer of @auricas limited, says, 'a multi-million pound branding strategy can be seriously undermined simply by a visiting customer seeing a member of staff standing around, smoking outside the front door'. The investment in corporate image and branding can be so easily diminished by unprofessional staff, and this reputation will readily spread.

To consistently design, produce and market great products and services is a function of the corporate culture, but it is the *sustainability* of that standard that *gives* an organization a corporate culture, and one which a company should seek to reflect in its branding and to reinforce at every opportunity. The people of any organization form the cultural infrastructure of a company and, as such, have the ability to demonstrate the corporate identity much more powerfully than any logo or website. In studies of companies and what makes them more successful than others, it is the 'soft' elements that make them different – that is, the people, the way they behave and communicate internally and externally; the social centric of the organization. Anyone can reproduce a product or provide a similar type of service. Many have tried to imitate the products of Microsoft, for example, but it would be nearly impossible to create the same culture. The 'soft' or 'human' element of the corporate brand is the portion that makes the company unique, that provides its biggest differentiator and that can ultimately make it more successful than its competitors. In a survey of chief executive officers (CEOs) and personnel directors from Fortune 1000 companies, it was found that 86 per cent agreed that they could project a better corporate image to their clients. Recent research among senior directors and CEOs for this book backs up previous study findings that good communications skills (presentation skills, telephone manner, and clear articulation and writing) were consistently considered the most important factor when recruiting and promoting staff. Ranked next in importance was personal presentation, which includes grooming (personal hygiene, teeth, hair, skin), appearance (dress, fitness, style) and manners. These two areas were rated higher than an MBA qualification. This is not to say that an MBA is not important, but rather that people communication skills, verbal and non-verbal, provide a greater differentiator for the organization, thereby creating powerful competition. All of the respondents from these top companies also believed that the corporate image had a direct impact on their profitability. It is amazing, then, that although more companies than ever are now providing training in image for their staff, there is still a high percentage that do not.

Matching Expectations

Have you ever built up expectations of a company only to have your illusions shattered when you meet the representative of that company for the first time? I'm sure you have many times over. When we are faced with a well-groomed sales person, dressed appropriately and projecting positive physiology, subconsciously we immediately feel comfortable with the company because we have trust in its professionalism. So, the fact remains that when dealing with people, whether it be sales person, customer service staff or management, who command respect and trust and portray professionalism, we are far more likely to buy from or buy into that company and feel good about it.

Example 1

Meeting the Expectation

A client recounted a situation that happened to them. They were seeking to award a management consultancy contract for an internal project, and invited two companies to present their proposals. One of these companies was the well-known PricewaterhouseCoopers (formerly Price Waterhouse and Coopers & Lybrand), the other was a smaller, lesser-known company. The first to make their presentation were two sales executives from the smaller company, who, let's face it, had a great opportunity to win against their larger competitor. Both of the companies had been recommended, and my client had received good-quality literature from both, setting an expected level of professionalism. When these two men arrived, they looked, in my client's words, 'like they'd travelled for a few hours in their suits and had a sleep on the way'! Their jackets and trousers were creased and one of them had left the top button of his shirt undone, with a distinct gap above the knot of his tired-looking tie. Their presentation was unrehearsed, which was apparent from their lack of familiarity with the slides. PwC, on the other hand, had prepared professional documents with the client's logo on the front, and their presentation was slick and professional. They looked the part in smart, well-fitted suits, with leather folders and quality pens.

The outcome of this session: despite its consultancy fees being significantly higher than those of its competitors, PwC won the contract hands down. Of course, this valuable contract was lost not just because the other company was *ill prepared*, but for two reasons: first, it gave out valuable clues to its potential client about its approach to business generally. Not only had the sales executives portrayed sloppy messages about themselves, they had created an image of their company which suggested questionable quality standards, unreliability, lack of customer care and had imparted a strong desire not to be associated with the company. The client was not given the impression that this company could fulfil its requirements in terms of quality and service. At that time, the sales executives were the face of their company – their company personified. Second, and on the other hand, PwC presented a professional image, totally in line with expectations. The client was not disappointed and was content to pay the higher price for peace of mind and for perceived reliability and trust. According to research, companies noted for outstanding quality and service charge fees that are, on average, 9 per cent higher. All of this clearly illustrates the damage that can be inflicted when perceptions are negative and the benefits when they're positive.

Example 2

Creating a Distraction

Another client told of an experience they had when a female sales director presented her company's software to them. This software company had also been recommended to my client. The sales director chose to make her presentation to her audience of all three directors and several senior staff, with no jacket on. She also wore a pastel-coloured blouse, which buttoned down the front and unfortunately was not a good fit – hence, it gaped across her chest. Her hair was also hanging over her face, in an unkempt, fluffy style. The audience felt uncomfortable and embarrassed for the presenter, combined with genuine sympathy for her – not an ideal way to attempt to win business! She had obviously created a distraction by her appearance; and, as a result, the audience were not focusing 100 per cent on the presentation and content.

In an internal meeting with staff after the presentation, the group decided that they just didn't feel that this company would be right for them. Being a relatively small firm they needed a totally reliable supplier who could deliver and implement to agreed timescales and provide a high standard of after-sales service.

Again the quality messages just didn't come through and, as a senior representative of the company, this sales director had not been able to command respect for herself and her company and products to the extent that made my client trust them and want to do business with them. No matter how 'attractive' an image this woman presented to the men, joking aside, when it comes down to business a professional identity is paramount, and any underlying feelings of sloppiness and mistrust, no matter how they are portrayed, will have enormous impact on your overall perception. Whatever your reaction to this example, it is just further proof that you cannot afford to ignore the very real and convincing facts surrounding the impact of non-verbal communication.

So, consistency of the corporate brand is key. There are some organizations that are huge yet still manage to sustain the corporate brand. Take the Virgin Group – consistency is apparent throughout all Virgin businesses, from the red of the logo to the bubbly and friendly staff and creative approach to business. This of course stems from the personality of Sir Richard Branson at the top and is consistent throughout. The sustainability of the corporate brand is a major success factor for Virgin. If it does slip up, we're almost prepared to forgive Virgin because of the usual high level of branding consistency. Consistent lapses, on the other hand, will label a company as a liar and a cheat.

I wonder just how much business is lost by a lack of positive personification of the corporate brand, which is so expensive to build. Hundreds of thousands and sometimes millions of pounds a year is invested on corporate image, in terms of advertising, websites and office premises. Of course it is almost impossible to gauge, but we know from personal experience that if a company fails to meet our expectations, we lose trust and are less likely to deal with it. Research shows that one of the primary reasons why customers go elsewhere is their supplier's perceived neglect or indifference. You have to be aware that vital clues are given out not just about your personal brand values and your approach to business, but about the brand values of your company and its products and services too. If staff in an organization back up and reinforce the right messages about the corporate identity, an extremely powerful brand image is portrayed. Singapore Airlines hit success big time when it introduced, for real, 'The Singapore Girl' – the impeccably groomed, caring and feminine staff who the airline used to project the corporate image in advertisements. This approach personified the airline's key messages of friendliness, caring attitude and attention to detail, and reinforced its brand. The effect was a powerful consistency between advertising and actual customer experience. This paves the way for unsurpassed success every time. Think about the times you've been let down or disappointed by a company, whether it be a restaurant, hotel or perhaps after-sales service. How many times does this relate back to the human element? If only the *restaurant manager* had dealt with your complaint in a manner that would instil confidence in the organization's usual high-quality standards and in a way that would encourage you to go back, the negative attitude you had about that organization would be alleviated and the impact lessened. We all remember when we have received bad service, whether it be at work or in your home life, and more often than not it is down to the way we are treated by other people. Some alarming research shows that complaints about service have increased 400 per cent since 1983, and that 96 per cent of customers with problems never tell you they have a problem – they simply take their business elsewhere.

Corporate Personality

A company's vision, values, culture and daily operations form its unique personality, and every member of staff is part of that personality. Unlike smaller companies, many multi-national companies are so large that they do not have a perceived 'human' relationship with customers – for instance, we don't deal with Mr Texaco or Ms B&Q and, even though there may be a Dell within the company, we are unlikely to see him or her. Because companies like this have no meaningful and inter-personal relationship with customers (only the smaller businesses can do this), there is a danger of a non-caring culture being grown. The client-facing staff in any organization are vital to success – they are the differentiator and they can build human relationships with customers that the corporation as a whole cannot. Remember the old cliché, *the customer is king*. It is not about continually lowering prices – as customers, what we all want is a positive attitude, business with style and pleasant experiences. So it is that people are the element of branding that give a corporation an actual personality.

Corporate personality is not optional – you cannot decide to do without it. You will be perceived to have a personality anyway, and it may not be one you would choose. Some of the world's most successful companies have used real people to build their corporate brand. These people provide an attractive value to the product or service and represent a personality that customers would like to be associated with. Take Nike and Tiger Woods: young, fit, healthy and successful are key values being portrayed here – who doesn't want that?

If you manage people, it is time to think about the element of branding that is most likely to powerfully and consistently reinforce the desired messages – your staff. As an individual, there is nothing that will make more of a positive impact than ensuring that your audience feel respected, instilling trust and confidence in your audience and achieving this while creating a pleasant atmosphere for communication. Throughout the rest of the book I will provide clear guidelines on how to achieve this with your personal presentation.

Your Company's Image

Image represents the combined *perceptions* that customers have about a company – how people see you. It is the customer's perception rather than the company's intention which creates an image. So, let's consider your own environment. Give some thought to the image of the company you work for, whether it be a large multi-national or your own small business. What key messages are portrayed by the branding and advertising? Write some of them down. Here are some adjectives to help:

- Professional
- Creative
- Forward-thinking
- Dynamic
- Conservative
- Traditional

- Friendly
- Refreshing
- International
- Customer-centric
- Approachable
- Organized

- Quality
- Trustworthy
- Fun
- Reliable

Think about these values for a moment. Is there a synergy between these and the values presented to your clients? Are the values *always* reinforced by everything the company does internally and externally? It is unlikely that your answer will be 'yes', but it is important to strive towards this to achieve total consistency.

Quality Standards

Let us take the concept of 'quality'. We know that quality can be reflected in advertising and marketing collateral, but how does it declare itself in a person? In other words, how is it personified? In my workshops, people will say that quality = 'smart', so what does 'smart' mean; how is it defined? Some people might say a suit, others a tie, and still others clean shoes. The fact is, there is no one element, it has to be collective. For example, would a creased suit with the appearance of having been stored in a suitcase overnight but teamed with expensive leather and well-maintained shoes look 'quality'? Unfortunately, the shoes would be lost in a distraction of sloppiness. You don't necessarily need designer labels, but good-quality clothes, which fit well and suit your body shape, are essential. Your accessories also give messages of quality and show attention to detail.

What is Professional?

You might say, 'dark suit and tie', or perhaps 'looking confident'. There can be no one answer, only solid guidelines. Every situation is different, as is every person and their approach. What is certain, however, is that

Professional = Being Appropriate.

'Appropriate' Factors

Your audience and their expectations

The situation and the environment

Your objectives

Your industry

You should consider all of these elements and then decide what dress code, behaviour and approach are appropriate. You need to find out as much as possible about each factor. We're all used to asking what the dress code is for a private dinner, for example (so as not to look out of place, over-dressed or under-dressed), but we are not so good when it comes to business situations. What I want to establish here is that you must always bring these factors to the fore when considering your approach. There are no rules, just guidelines, and it is also important that your personality and individuality should still be apparent, to an appropriate level. What is vital is that you always look professional and credible by ensuring that your standard of grooming is high, your posture sharp and your body language appropriate.

Creative Flair

If this is an important corporate or personal branding message for you, then words alone will not create the message. You need to show some flair with your clothes, and colour plays an important part here. Both women and men should avoid the conservative and safe plain dark suit and white shirt. Navy is also considered to be safe and is lacking in creativity. If you fail to display flair, you'll be branded as conservative and unimaginative.

Approachable and Friendly

You will not achieve this in a dark and sombre suit – lighter colours are far more approachable when you want to win friends and influence people. For example, a grey suit is considered to be much more 'user-friendly' than a navy one, so I would always recommend wearing a grey suit when you really need people to open up and communicate. For my image workshops, I usually get delegates to complete a questionnaire with colleagues prior to the session. They have to ask a colleague or boss how they come across when meeting people for the first time. A woman who attended one of my workshops was shocked to hear that she gave the illusion of being slightly aloof and unapproachable. She was adamant that this was not her character at all. When you learn that she was wearing black from head to toe, had striking silvery-grey hair and wore no make-up, it should be clear why she was branded in this way. In the session, I gave her ideas about what to wear with her beloved black, how to soften her look and demonstrated a natural yet uplifting make-over on her. The effect was incredible – she now fully understands the power of non-verbal communication and personal appearance. She has learned that appearances *can* get in the way of projecting true qualities and is grateful for having this pointed out to her. She now teams her black with more flattering colours and she smiles more!

Forward-thinking

Most companies and industries will want to portray a forward-thinking culture, with perhaps the exception of those organizations that thrive on traditionalism and history for their success. However, even many of these will still want their clients to perceive them as forward thinking in business process terms. So, it is time to stop wearing those conservative clothes, to chuck out those dated, boxy, double-breasted suits you have had for a few years, or those brass-buttoned blazers, ladies! One thing you cannot afford to do is to look dated. If you look a bit 1990s (or worse!) and out of touch, your thought processes and approach will be considered to be out of touch too.

Trust Me!

As we saw in the example with PwC earlier, it is easy to jeopardize others' trust in you and your company to do the job in hand to the quality standards required. We have to command trust from our audience in order for them to believe us and take on board what we are saying. Words alone cannot achieve this – in fact, the very words 'trust me' conjure up feelings of insincerity. Building trust is vital if we are to be successful, and we can do this in a number of ways. Reliability is a key one – doing what we say we are going to do and when. But when it comes to personal presentation and communication there are a number of elements to consider with regard to body language and dress.

Bad 'Corporate' Manners

It is an undeniably depressing fact that today we almost take for granted that nobody will return our call, send that information we asked for or meet that deadline without a shower of excuses. What is happening to our manners? The fact is that while this state of affairs can damage the corporate professional reputation, it is doing immense damage to *your* image and the way people perceive *you*. You will be labelled inefficient, not in control, lazy, a bad time manager and rude, by not doing something you said you were going to do. Nobody likes to have to chase people, or has the time to, and you will be branded an irritation at best and exceptionally rude at worst. A colleague of mine has recently compiled a presentation on corporate good manners – it's a shame that he has highlighted a need for an entire presentation on the subject.

Sadly, then, bad manners are being accepted as the 'way it is in business today'. So, if it is so unusual to display good manners, what better opportunity for you to make a huge positive impact on your contacts? Always do what you say you're going to do and when you say you're going to do it by, unless there is some exceptional reason why, and I mean exceptional. It is so refreshing to communicate with people who are efficient, and they will always stand very high in my estimation. Since 2000 I have had the great fortune to work with a person who has restored my belief in human trust and efficiency. Sue, who has taken on a PR and marketing role for me, is held in extremely high regard among all of her clients, which is due not least to her total reliability in doing what she says she is going to do. People like Sue will always be in demand, refreshing to work with, and held in high esteem in business.

Corporate Good Manners – Tips

Always return a call – call out of hours if necessary and leave a voicemail

A quick 'thank you' email when appropriate will win you serious respect

Always do what you say you are going to do and when you said you would do it by

Set realistic expectations so that you are not in danger of not meeting them

To Dress Down or not to Dress Down – Brand Inconsistency?

I wonder just how many times this has crossed your mind and that of your colleagues! Since the dress-down phenomenon started in Silicon Valley in the US in the early 1980s, it has swept the business world, and many organizations, if not most, have now tried out the trend. Many have even gone full circle and returned to being 'suited' in the office. Many companies, such as Arthur Andersen, which famously announced a dress-down code in 1999, state now that their policy is flexible and open for people to wear suits or dress down. I believe that much of the reversal of the trend is down to companies not having implemented it properly to start with, with no real standards being established from day one. They have found that because dress down is so ambiguous and wide open to misinterpretation, a loss of corporate consistency has been created, which in turn has jeopardized the corporate brand. Many senior managers have reverted to wearing suits because they feel they have a loss of power, authority and credibility without the armour of their jacket. When consistency is key to corporate branding, a clear standard of dress code has to be considered a major element.

Your Window Display

So, you see, whatever the corporate values of your company, it is essential to personify these key messages in the way that you and your staff portray yourselves to the outside world. You are the 'window display' of your business, and you need to ensure that this entices customers closer to doing business with you. This is especially important if your business relies on outside agencies, outlets or subcontractors to provide a service to your clients. The potential dangers of this were particularly apparent to me recently when attending an exhibition. I could not help but notice a woman on a stand for a financial investment company, and was astonished at her personal presentation. She was dressed in inappropriate clothes, her hair hung over her unmade-up face and I don't think she had mastered the act of smiling! I could not resist striking up a conversation with her (during which her stale breath added to the impact), and on enquiring what her job was she told me that she did not work for the financial company but for an agency representing it. The financial company exhibiting would have no idea how unprofessionally its organization was being portrayed by one person who really could not give a hoot about the sloppy messages she was presenting. In my eyes, and I am sure in several hundred others, this company had lost serious credibility. With a lapse like this when you're setting out your 'window display', you are in real danger of losing the critical consistency that branding requires in order for you to be increasingly successful in a competitive world.

chapter 2

How is my Image?

YOU HAVE NOW SEEN THE BENEFITS OF maintaining consistency within a corporate brand, and the importance of the people element being in synergy with that brand, so now for some really *personal* stuff. If you want to improve your personal power and impact, you first need to look at the image you currently present and establish what you like about it, what you do not like, what works and what doesn't. Because, no matter how powerful and assertive you may feel inside, it is the non-verbal messages you give out that can initially propel you forward to greater success, and without which you could get left behind in a competitive environment.

An easy way to explain personal image is to use the 'Johari window', which was developed by two psychologists, Joseph Luft and Harry Ingham. It makes the process of understanding yourself clearer and easier to achieve, and provides a great basis for improving the impact you make on others.

Public self	**Blind spots**
Private self	**Unknown self**

The Public self is the part of you that you are happy and confident about showing to the world. It is the part that everybody knows and understands about you. The Private self is the part that only you know about – the elements of you that you are not necessarily happy to share with others, but it can also contain your goals and your dreams. Only your closest friends and family get a look at the Private self. We all have Blind spots – these are the parts that others see about you but that you cannot see about yourself. Last, there is the Unknown self, the untapped area of your personal potential which is unknown to you and to others.

With the aim of improving your personal image you need to look first at the Private self and tap into areas of your personality – what do you want to achieve and what do you want to project to others? Then, by looking at your Public self and your Blind spots, you can establish those elements of your appearance and behaviour that are working towards this goal and those that are holding you back. By becoming aware of the Blind spots, both negative and positive, you can improve your projected image, personal power and inner confidence. Having analysed the Public self and Blind spots, you can start to uncover the Unknown self and to unlock some of the unknown potential you have for enhancing your personal image. Before going any further, you need to be aware that there are no rights and wrongs to a projected image, just guidelines, levels of appropriateness and socially accepted standards below which you are in danger of damaging your professional reputation and personal positive impact.

It is important to uncover your personal strengths as well as establishing the areas for improvement before you can begin to determine a way forward to achieving greater personal power. In much the same way as companies have to keep pace with a changing world by rebranding and redefining strategies, we too have to keep reassessing and rebranding ourselves. Have you noticed how often we see B-list celebrities reinventing themselves when they are not getting the exposure they want and need? They often go through a complete image overhaul, sometimes for the better, sometimes not, but it usually achieves the desired objective of greater media coverage. Although some politicians will insist that they are not interested in image, and some will say that image is superficial, you can be sure that they know that no matter what they say, just like anybody in the public eye, they will be judged by their appearance. But rebranding ourselves does not just mean changing seemingly superficial things such as clothing styles, colours and hairstyles; it means adopting new attitudes and behaviour in order not to alienate ourselves in a changing environment. The way you present yourself to the world is your own *personal advertisement*, more effective than any business card or brochure. As we all know, jobs for life no longer exist, so we have to keep reinventing ourselves in order to survive, let alone thrive, in the business world of the 21st century. What is for sure is that work will always exist and that it's up to you to ensure that you make a powerful personal impact in all that you do to maximize your opportunities for exposure and greater success.

Be Individual

In this 21st-century environment, we are flooded with innovation and creativity. In business we see major brands working together to create powerful allegiances – for example, J. Sainsbury have introduced Boots health and beauty products into some larger Sainsbury supermarkets, and have formed a joint venture with Oddbins to provide an online wine service to customers. This kind of vision and creativity is vital in a hypercompetitive marketplace. As Marc Gobé says in his book *Emotional Branding*, '. . . we have reached this time when corporations clearly need to fine tune their focus on the consumer psyche and understand the importance of the constantly evolving trends in their consumers' lifestyles . . .' (Gobé, 2001: xvii). Among this creativity, we are seeing much more individualism than we have been used to over the past few decades – this is a refreshing modern development. It is prevalent not only in business but also in the way we decorate our homes, in the way we dress and in our desire to be unique with our own quirky ways among a group of friends. Generally, we are much more likely to want to stand out in a crowd nowadays. In fashion, we see new trends each season paraded on the catwalks and interpreted by the high-street stores, but, more than ever before, we are inclined to absorb these new creations and ideas, and to use them in ways that bring out our own personality and uniqueness, rather than be 'dictated' to about what to wear and what not to wear to be in vogue. Personality and individualism play a major part in the way we dress in the modern world, and contemporary today can mean not just the latest designs but perhaps a mixture of retro, high fashion and personal creativity. We are less likely to have our hair styled the same way as the new girl in the office just because it looks great on her, or buy a red car just like John's down the road, but we are more likely to think about what we could do differently in order to bring out our unique personality more. In other words, we observe what is going on around us and use it to enhance our own individualism. The world today is not about keeping up with the Joneses, but is about absorbing all the options available to us and deciding what is right for us and our environment. What do we feel comfortable with – what works for us? We're getting better at saying, 'no, that's not for me, but this is'. Your own Personal Brand Values (PBVs) are a major element in creating personal impact. They give you a powerful uniqueness. Nothing is as visually persuasive as yourself, and your uniqueness is your major differentiator in a world of competition and change. As Sir Richard Branson says, 'Personality is crucial and just as important as qualifications'. The aim of this chapter is to help you discover and use your personality and individualism on the road to creating your own unique and positive brand image.

Being Appropriate and Meeting Expectations

In the last chapter we looked at personifying the corporate brand in terms of quality of personal image, creativity and how being professional equals being appropriate. We should now look at the elements of being *appropriate*, and what you need to consider to achieve this. Part of being appropriately presented is being in touch with your audience and establishing what their expectations are, otherwise you are in danger of creating negative impact. Of course, when portraying an image, it is your audience, whether one person or a large group, to whom you are giving out clues about yourself. This audience will often have formed an impression of you and your company before meeting you. This may have been from marketing collateral, advertising or recommendation, or, of course, they may have met you before. They will therefore have formed an unconscious expectation of your appearance and approach. I can certainly relate to this – being an image consultant, everybody, without doubt, conjures up an image of me in advance of meeting me, and I hope are pleasantly surprised to find I am not actually stuck in the 1980s, always decked out in perfectly coordinated clothes, with heavy make-up and carrying a bag full of colourful scarves! We image consultants fall into the stereotype trap just as other professionals do. But if a negative stereotype does exist, you have a great opportunity to exert positive impact by shattering the stereotype and exceeding the expectation. What is interesting too is that in many of my meetings and workshops, people admit during the session that they paid more attention to their outfit and grooming that day, knowing they were meeting an 'image consultant', thinking that they would be scrutinized – and they're probably right! But this is not just because image is my job – you do it too, albeit often subconsciously. Take this example: you are meeting with the web designer from a design company and you may quite reasonably expect to see:

- A young and dynamic person
- Sharpness
- Vitality
- Creative and/or contemporary clothes
- Friendly and relaxed physiology

When you see, for example, a much older person, conservatively dressed in a dated suit, who seems quiet and under-confident and whose body language is closed and defensive, you quite understandably start to subconsciously question their creative and technical skills, their ability to think diversely and their forward-thinking capabilities, which are precisely the skills you are paying this company large sums of money for. They will not have met your initial expectations, and doubts will start to form. This is an extreme example, but we do equate what we see with actual perceived ability – we believe what we see. It is often said that what we see on the outside is a reflection of inner values, and, in the words of Aristotle, 'we are what we continually do'. In this example the image of the web designer could have been getting in the way of portraying true qualities. Whether you accept this scenario as right and just, or not, the fact remains that research and studies categorically and consistently reinforce that the non-verbal messages present a stronger and more believable message every time. It is initially the outer packaging that inspires trust and that commands respect, or lack of it, every time.

When we're assessing what is appropriate dress code and behaviour, we need to consider the situation and environment too. If you're able to choose the environment for a meeting or presentation, then use this to your advantage. Setting an appropriate atmosphere wherever possible will be conducive to effective communication, and you have another opportunity to reinforce your corporate image and your own personal impact. Choosing an outfit that suits the environment is important – for example, what is appropriate for a contract negotiation with a client, where some authority is required, is probably not appropriate for a team-building session, where a more relaxed approach is needed for encouraging open discussion. In a business situation you cannot afford to look out of place. Although there are no rights and wrongs, considering an appropriate dress code for the situation and the client is crucial if you are to encourage effective communication from the outset. If, for example, you are under-dressed in smart/casual clothes and your client is formally dressed in a suit, both of you could feel uncomfortable. Of course, nine times out of ten in a business situation it will be obvious that a suit or jacket is required, but be careful not to let that one occasion when you have not given enough consideration to the situation and environment to damage your image.

If you are to create the personal power you desire, your objectives should be an important consideration for every situation you find yourself in. For example, if your aim is to come away with that contract signed or that 'buy in' to your idea, then you will need to consider what style of clothing is going to give you added authority, integrity and credibility. Do not lose sight of what you want from a situation – from an in-depth and open discussion to forming the foundations of a long-term business relationship, your personal appearance is vital to achieving this.

First Things First

The first step on the road to improving personal image and impact is thinking about how you *believe* you come across – in other words, the image you think you portray. You need to ascertain your personal strengths or your Personal Brand Values (PBVs), and you also need to be aware of your weaknesses and areas for improvement – the elements of your image that could be getting in the way of projecting your true values and abilities. Be your own critic. You need to start by thinking about how you present yourself to the world and how the world sees you. In other words, what perceptions do you think people have about you? Your image is the result of the collective perceptions people have about you, which are projected through your appearance, behaviour, gestures, facial expressions and voice – your 'personal package'. By the end of this chapter you will be clear about your PBVs and those areas you need to brush up on.

When you have completed this chapter, you will have visited areas that perhaps you've not even thought about before, or at least not since your very first job interview. So often we forget some of the basic elements that can let us down. Stop and think for a moment about how you judge other people within the first 30 seconds of meeting them. The key things you will have subconsciously noted will be their socio-economic group, the colour of their skin, their age and sex, and how professional, efficient, reliable, successful, trustworthy, honest and credible they are. Well, guess what, other people will judge you in this way too. Pretty obvious, isn't it, but just how often do you stop and think about this powerful tool you have available to you for increasing personal impact? In a recent presentation to 150 senior chartered accountants, I asked, 'how many of you have had feedback on your handshake?' Not one person in the room had ever been told how their handshake came across, so how did they know the impact they were making in those first few vital seconds? I can tell you that when sampling a few handshakes in an exercise that followed, a significant number of those accountants had a problem, which they were totally unaware of until that time. This neglect and lack of knowledge about the image we portray is not uncommon and it is potentially damaging to our personal brand.

The Selling Game

Whatever we do in life, the fact is that we are all in the selling business, either directly or indirectly, as we are in effect 'selling' ourselves all of the time. So, you must find your own strengths and PBVs in order to make people want to 'buy into' you and hear more from you. We give out vital clues about ourselves and our product or service by the way we choose to present ourselves to our audience, whether that audience is one person or a large group. We non-verbally 'tell' people how efficient we are, how capable, creative and professional, by our personal presentation and physiology. And, much like a window display, we have to make sure that our PBVs are 'seen' by the audience and not screened by a distraction elsewhere in our personal presentation.

First Impressions Last

A good place to start is by looking at the first impression you genuinely think you create. People not only make judgements about us from the clues we give them through our 'personal package', but they do this within seconds of meeting us. Before you can improve, you need to *really* think about the impression you create and the one you would like to create. Remember that old cliché, 'you never get a second chance to make a first impression' – it's so very true.

The process we are going to use in this book to improve personal image impact is one of

Assess → Feedback → Action

This process is cyclical in that you should continually assess, obtain feedback, take action and assess again to improve wherever possible. We should never feel that we are so good at something that feedback is no longer essential. We can always be better than before – we are evolving, and we should keep reinventing ourselves.

Step 1 – Assess

Assessing How You Come Across in the First 30 Seconds

The idea of this exercise is to help you to take a good, hard look at yourself and to assess how you think you are perceived by others on first meeting. It is important that you are as honest as possible. Try to imagine a 3-second advert of yourself and think about how you come across. Tick or highlight the adjectives and phrases that you feel best describe you – add some of your own if necessary, but make sure you *really* think about each question.

How would you describe yourself in each of these areas?

1. Handshake

    - Strong
    - Wet fish
    - Firm
    - Weak
    - Direct
    - Dominating
    - Limp
    - Ineffectual

2. Posture

    - Upright
    - Sloppy
    - Natural
    - Comfortable
    - Confident
    - Sloped shoulders
    - Stiff

3. Smiling

    - I find it easy to smile when meeting people
    - I feel self-conscious because my teeth need attention
    - I never smile in a business situation
    - It doesn't feel natural

4. Eye contact

    - Direct
    - I blink a lot
    - Maintained
    - Intermittent
    - Fleeting

5. Shoes

    - Well maintained
    - Expensive
    - Practical
    - Polished
    - Classic styles
    - Comfortable, if not stylish
    - A little dated

6. Dress style

- Natural and comfortable
- 'It'll do for work' attitude
- Not bothered about fashion
- Uncomfortable in a suit

- Well co-ordinated and stylish
- Always appropriate
- Classic
- Creative

7. Grooming

- Lapse for work
- Always wear make-up for work (women)
- I always do a full-length check in the mirror before leaving the house
- Shower every morning

- Don't shave on dress-down days
- Never wear worn or stained clothes
- Always immaculate
- Clothes fit well

8. Voice

- Soft
- Well paced
- Distinctive
- High-pitched
- Monotone

- Strong
- Strong accent
- Loud
- Lacks clarity
- Powerful

9. Physical fitness

- Questionable
- No time to pay attention to fitness

- First rate
- I get out of breath easily
- Exercise wherever possible

10. Remembering people's names

- I always forget
- I often get names wrong

- I have a method of remembering names

11. The colours I generally wear

- Bright and clear
- Bold and contrasting
- Safe and conservative
- Flattering for me

- Neutral (black, white, grey, brown, navy)
- No idea which colours make me look sharp and healthy

12. Small talk

- Can always strike up a conversation
- I'm easy to talk to

- I find small talk difficult
- I always have lots of subjects I can talk about

So, now you have thought long and hard about your Public self, you will have uncovered some things you do well and others that need attention. You need to start recording these on a Personal Image Action Plan. Devise your own from the example below and add more lines where necessary. By recording this information you will start to highlight your PBVs too – your personal strengths. Use the Personal Brand Value section for this. To enhance your PBVs, think about some of the really positive things people say about you – for example, you are always lively, or reliable, can always cheer people up, make people feel comfortable and so on, and record these. This is a wonderful confidence-boosting exercise, and you should keep these strengths visible on your desk or in your drawer to look at on a daily basis.

Step 2 – Feedback

Now is the time to try to examine those Blind spots – these are the parts that you are not aware of but others are. The best way to do this is to ask colleagues, your boss or friends for feedback using the questionnaire you have just completed. See how they think you come across in each of these areas. Be aware that friends may not be the

My Personal Image Action Plan

My strengths on meeting people for the first time are:

1. _____
2. _____
3. _____

Areas I need to improve are:

1. _____
2. _____
3. _____

Actions to be taken to achieve improvement

_____

_____

Dated

_____

My Personal Brand Values

1. _____
2. _____
3. _____
4. _____
5. _____

Keep this form visible on a daily basis.

best people to ask – they may not be as objective as you need. Explain that you are evaluating your image and how others perceive you and in order to be helpful they need to give you honest answers. When you have these responses, compare them with your own perceptions. You may have some pleasant surprises and some not so welcome ones! The positive aspects should become PBVs and go on your list of strengths, the negative ones must go on the action plan to do something about. So, update your Personal Image Action Plan and make a personal commitment to be 100 per cent aware of your PBVs and capitalize on them, and to address the areas needing attention. The rest of this book will focus on how to improve in these areas. You can also use the following questions to gain feedback. I know this exercise is tough, but it is the most effective way to gain insight into how the world sees you so that you can move forward with added confidence.

1. What kind of image do I project?

2. What impression do I make on strangers upon meeting?

3. How do clients react towards me?

4. What one behavioural trait might be worth changing?

5. What recommendations do you have about my appearance to project a better image?

You should revisit this questionnaire one to two months after reading this book, and at regular intervals thereafter, to see how you've improved. Also continue to get feedback from a different set of colleagues.

Having completed this exercise, now start to revisit your Private self and list the values that are important to you and that you really want to portray to others. Some suggested words might be:

- Creative
- Attractive
- Forward-thinking
- Dynamic
- Relaxed
- Upbeat
- Reliable

- Powerful
- Considerate
- Efficient
- Successful
- Credible
- Sharp
- Elegant

- Approachable
- Professional
- Dramatic
- Helpful
- Stylish
- Versatile
- Modern

What do I already portray?

_____

_____

_____

What needs more work?

_____

_____

_____

Step 3 – Action

And now it is time to take **Step 3 – Action**. The rest of this book will provide you with guidelines to improve your image. As you read through, make notes on areas that you know will help you to improve and add to your Personal Image Action Plan too.

chapter 3

Your Personal 'Package'

EVERY MESSAGE NEEDS A MEDIUM TO present it with impact – your messages of personal values, standards, abilities – in fact, what you stand for – will be strongly projected through your personal image and how you present yourself. Just as companies spend millions of pounds on packaging and marketing to attract us to a product and make us want to buy it, you must invest effort in your own personal presentation to 'sell' yourself and to make others want to discover more about what is inside. Grooming and clothes are the 'packaging' of your total image. This chapter will concentrate on the non-verbal aspects of communication – that is, your appearance in terms of dress and grooming – and how to make those unspoken messages work *for* you and propel you towards creating greater image impact, personal power and success. You've only got to remember Julia Roberts' boutique scene in the hit film *Pretty Woman* to understand the power of dress and grooming in gaining respect and achieving what you want. Tom Peters, author of *In Search of Excellence*, said, 'If you aren't being seen you won't get on' (Peters, 1995). You can make sure that you stand out from the crowd by the way you *package* yourself.

You have now discovered your Personal Brand Values (PBVs) and have a greater understanding of your self-image and the image you already portray. Much of this projected image is received by others in the first 30 seconds of meeting them, and more than 50 per cent is apportioned to your non-verbal communication – that is, your appearance and body language. On first impressions, only about 7 per cent of the impact you make is related to the actual words you use, with 38 per cent related to voice quality. These percentages are the result of research carried out by social psychologist Professor Albert Mehrabian, from the University of California in Los Angeles. Some argue that these figures are slightly flawed as they were carried out with students and in the 1970s, but, even if we were to treble the figures, the impact our words have on the way we are judged initially still only represents less than 25 per cent of the message portrayed. The figures show that, initially, we are more likely to believe what we *see* rather than what we *hear*. If you look the part and your body language is consistent, then your words will be reinforced and your audience will be more likely to trust what you're saying and want to hear more. So, it is important to get your personal presentation right first time. It is hard work to correct an unfortunate first impression – in fact, research shows that it takes 21 further experiences to change a first impression. Of course, a positive first impression must be consistently maintained and backed up with actual delivery in order to build effective and successful relationships, and while a positive impact initially will not guarantee success, without it you can almost guarantee failure. This book is designed to help you to improve your personal image and consequently to provide you with a platform from which you can continually develop your new-found skills to maintain a consistent positive impact and image throughout your career and personal life.

You need to consider your *whole* image in order to create positive impact – one element alone will not ensure credibility. For example, if your dress and grooming are immaculate but when you open your mouth your speech is monotone and unclear or has nervous overtones, you will present an inconsistent message and your audience will be confused and possibly lost.

So, hold on tight, now is the time to start out on the fast track to implementing those all-important improvements to your personal presentation. In this chapter we will cover appearance and dress sense; body language will be covered in Chapter 5; and voice impact will be examined in Chapter 6. You will see just how important your outer packaging is and how to avoid wrecking your image in those vital first few seconds. We know that everybody makes choices about their grooming and clothing deliberately, therefore we assume that these two elements say a great deal about us. It has been said that clothing is a visual reflection of the mind. We assume that the type of decisions we have made about our appearance reflect and indicate how we see ourselves and the level of our self-esteem. So, it is vital that we make sure that our appearance says what we want it to say about us as individuals and that we learn to recognize when it doesn't.

We all seek to be well dressed and professional in our working lives. In order to achieve this we have to remember five key elements about our appearance:

The well-dressed businessman or woman wears clothes that:

- complement them physically
- reflect their personality
- are current (not necessarily trendy)
- are appropriate for the situation and environment

. . . and is, above all, well groomed.

By considering these areas you are well on the way to improving your personal power.

Before we proceed with the keys to unlock personal power with appearance and dress, let's first of all look at a potential danger zone – the 'dated image'. One of the biggest image wreckers in today's fast-moving and cutting-edge business world is a dated appearance, which in turn can suggest dated thought processes and a dated approach to business. Check yours out on p. 42.

If you have answered 'yes' to any of these questions, then you could be in danger of damaging your positive image impact with a dated look from time to time or regularly. Now is the time to update.

There are key elements that can give a dated appearance – look for them in your wardrobe and check they still reflect current trends:

- Lapel width.
- Buttoning styles.
- Trouser width.
- Back vents.
- Pocket styles.
- Jacket length.

It makes sense to split part of this chapter into components for men and for women. First of all we'll deal with those elements common to both. At the end of the chapter, I'll cover colour impact for men and women, and key tips to creating a perfect business image. So, first, some common elements of personal image.

Good Fit

Anybody who has attended one of my workshops will know that bad fit is one of my pet hates. There is no need for it, it ruins a good outfit and it just serves to totally destroy any positive impact you hoped to make with your appearance. At best it looks like you've outgrown the garment or lost weight, and at worst it looks like a cheap bargain or a

Is Your Image Dating You?

Men	Women

1. Do you have any jackets/suits in your wardrobe that are more than 5 years old?
2. Do you tend to stick to your old favourite tie designs rather than buy new designs that reflect new trends?
3. Do you have a hairstyle that hasn't changed for more than 5 years? (Presuming, of course, that you have enough to do something with and, by the way, many women find baldness attractive!)
4. Is it more than 3 years since you updated your spectacle frames?
5. Do you sport a beard or moustache that has been pretty much the same for as long as you can remember?
6. Does your mobile phone outsize everybody else's?
7. Is your briefcase old and battered and look like it's been around for a number of years?

1. Is it more than 3 years since you've updated your make-up techniques and colours?
2. Do you own a brass-buttoned blazer?
3. Is it more than 3 years since you changed your hairstyle?
4. Do you always buy from similar shops rather than think outside the boxes and go for something a little different occasionally?
5. Do you wear similar colours each season and ignore fashion trends?
6. Does your accessory drawer look sparse or the same as it has done for a few years?
7. Do you tend to match shoes to belts and/or handbags?
8. Have you always avoided hair colour even though the grey is showing through?
9. Do you have pairs of shoes that you've owned for more than 5 years?

Men	Women
8. Is your watch design and strap looking a bit behind the times?	10. Are you still wearing navy tights?
9. Do you consider your brass-buttoned blazer a staple for smart/casual?	11. Have your scarves been around for a while or do you wear a scarf with everything?
10. Do you stick to white shirts come what may?	12. Is your jewellery the same style no matter what you're wearing or do you wear the same pieces all the time?
11. Do you have one pair of shoes for every business outfit?	
12. Do you over-do the jewellery a little (rings, an earring etc.), and does medallion man spring to mind?	

hand-me-down. I think you've got the message! Your clothes should look like an extension of you. So, step 1, get yourself a good seamstress, who you know will make good-quality alterations for you. You can, of course, use the service offered by many stores too, some of whom offer a free service for cardholders. If you are not a typical size – for example, I am a size 13 on the bottom half (accurate at time of writing but liable to change by the time I finish this book!) – then always opt for the next size up (I know it's hard), and get it altered to fit. A half-size too small will make you look a whole size bigger. Do make sure that your seams hang straight and are not pulled in any way. Having worked with many companies I can quite comfortably say that bad fit is one of the most commonly overlooked aspects of dress. I have also worked with many companies where staff wear uniforms, and good fit is often a problem here too. Whatever the outfit, uniform or suit, you will not look well presented and well groomed if your clothes fit badly. Don't undermine your positive impact with sloppy, ill-fitting clothes – it is just not worth it.

The Goal: An Elegantly Loose Fit

Jackets and coats – check the fit on the shoulders. They should fit exactly, without extending more than 2 cm past. I know this is sometimes a problem for women with fuller busts, as they need the width in the bust area, but a good seamstress will be able to alter the shoulders to fit. Always check the back of the jacket and ask for mirrors to do so if you have nobody with you to give you advice. There should be no vertical folds at the back, which suggest that the jacket is too big, and no horizontal folds, which mean it is too tight. The sleeves should end at the top of the thumb – any shorter or longer and they look ridiculous. The jacket must look perfect when buttoned too, and pockets should remain closed and not gaping. Make sure the jacket lapels lie flat.

Trousers and skirts – always allow about 3–4 cm either side at the seams for good fit and ease of movement. Underwear should never be visible because of tightness of clothes. Trousers and skirts should not curve in excessively underneath the bottom, but should hang naturally – unless they are jean-style, of course. For women, if you are very petite or very long in the leg then you may have difficulty finding trousers to fit well. I have included a few recommended suppliers at the back of the book. Make sure your trousers are the correct length – it is a common mistake for women to wear them too short. They should almost cover the top of the foot and be a maximum of 4 cm from the ground at the back of the heel, depending on the height of the heel. Too short on taller women and they look silly, and on petite women they will make you look shorter still. Always take the shoes you are likely to be wearing with the garment with you when visiting the seamstress. For men, your trousers should break only once on to your shoes and no more – remember Charlie Chaplin wanted to look ridiculous! If pockets stick out at all, then get them stitched in.

Avoid skirts that finish on the widest point of your calf – it is a very unflattering length and will make your legs look wider. It is better to go just above or just below the knee or down to the narrowing of the calf. For short skirts and skirts with a slit, do the comfort test by sitting down in it before you buy to test how much unwanted leg exposure there is. You could end up fidgeting with the skirt all the time.

Dresses – You should have 8 cm at either side at the seams to allow ease of movement while remaining a good fit. Most women are a different size top and bottom, and dresses that fit well are often hard to find. If you have this problem, then I recommend buying a size larger and having it altered to fit exactly.

Eyewear

Spectacles are now considered a fashion accessory – I know people who love them so much that they wear them with plain glass. You can express personality with your specs, perhaps more safely than with other items of clothing and accessories, and you can own several pairs for different looks and occasions. Thanks to designers such as Armani and Gucci we now have some incredibly stylish frames to choose from. Essential tip – if you haven't changed your spec frames in the past 5 years, do so without further delay. Even if you only wear sunglasses, they could be costing you dearly by giving you a dated image. If you wear specs all the time they are a very important aspect of your image. Our eyes feature prominently in our communication, so it is crucial that the style, colour and fit are right for you and your face shape. Take somebody with you to choose the frames – they will be able to give you an objective opinion.

Spec Tips

- Most high-street opticians, for example Dolland & Aitchison, now have great techniques for helping you to choose frames to suit your colouring and face shape.

- If you have a long nose, go for a lower bridge – too high a bridge will make the nose appear longer.

- Avoid tinted or transition lenses (those that darken in bright light) as these can obscure your eyes and make communication difficult and uncomfortable for your audience. Go for non-reflective lenses, too, which are coated in diamond quartz to cause less reflection, to ensure the eyes are visible.

- The colour of the frame is pretty much personal choice, but, if you have cool colouring (see section on Colour) you should generally opt for silver, pewter or black frames, and if you have warm colouring you should go for tortoiseshell, gold or brown frames. Of course, you could choose some wacky frames to be different too – it's up to you.

Smoking

I am going to be quite blunt here, because, although an emotive subject, it is crucial for all smokers to be aware of its impact. Smoking can be considered one of the biggest image wreckers of all. There are a number of reasons for this and it is important if you are a regular smoker that you take particular note of these areas. Not only can smoking discolour teeth and cause bad breath, it gives the skin a sallow and unhealthy look and promotes ageing lines around the mouth and eyes.

It can diminish your personal power due to these points alone, but it is safe to say that, to non-smokers particularly, any unpleasant indication that you do smoke could be negative too. Remember, the smell of smoke will also linger in your clothes and you may be completely unaware of this. Fabric fresheners such as Febreze are great for diminishing telltale odours. Freshen up your clothes if you have been in a smoky environment too.

Fitness

Although I do not advocate, given the busy lives you lead, that you should necessarily be at the height of physical fitness, I certainly do recommend that you exercise as much as possible, even if it is just using the stairs rather than the lift at the office. Without retaining a level of energy and vitality you could look drained and tired. To maintain positive image impact you need to look sharp and ready for business, to build credibility and make people want to deal with you. If you are significantly overweight, then be aware that this could get in the way of projecting your true qualities and abilities, so it would be sensible to address it. If you marked your fitness levels as a little questionable in the exercise in Chapter 2, then *do* something about it now. You'll feel better about yourself too.

Groom for Improvement

Having put a great deal of thought and effort into your wardrobe, don't blow it with lack of grooming. Your grooming habits are constantly visible, and research shows that the first things people remember about us are elements to do with grooming, rather than the specific clothes we are wearing. They remember the total image. When someone has a well-groomed appearance – clear skin, clean and pressed clothes, well-cut hair, looked-after teeth and hands, then they exude confidence and self-esteem. We assume, then, that they are well qualified to hold a senior position because of how they care about themselves. When we meet people our eyes quickly scan and take in the whole picture and then rest back on the face or the influencing triangle. This area is the triangular area with its point at the breastbone, coming up and out, covering the whole of the head. This is the part of the body with which we do most of our communicating and influencing. So, in a few seconds we have scanned the whole package and will quickly pick up on any negative distractions such as bad grooming. In a recent survey, an overwhelming 78 per cent of business professionals said that grooming had a direct impact on the perceived abilities of colleagues. Your personal grooming is probably one of the most convincing ways of destroying your personal power; this section aims to ensure that you achieve exactly the opposite result.

First of all, see how you score with your grooming:

Does your Grooming Make the Grade?

W = women only

M = men only

Do you get your shoes repaired only when the heels and soles have completely worn down?

Do you use shoe trees to keep your shoes in shape and from creasing across the top?

Do you ever polish your shoes when still warm – they absorb polish more effectively?

Do you wear different shoes to drive in to save the backs becoming scuffed?

Do you own a trouser press? (M)

When was the last time you took a close look at the state of your shirt or blouse collars?

Does your skin look healthy – do you use a regular skincare system?

Do you ever wear a tie or any other item of clothing that has a stain on it, just because you love wearing it and hope nobody will notice?

Do you always wear make-up to work, even on a dress down day? (W)

Do you always get your clothes altered where necessary to fit properly?

Do you always do a full-length check in the mirror before leaving for the office or an important meeting?

Do you hang your suit outside the wardrobe overnight after wearing to revive it?

Do your ever hang your suits outside to air?

Do you rotate your suits between wearing?

Do you always take off your jacket when travelling?

Do your nails tell the world you're a DIY enthusiast or stressed out?

Do you get your hair cut regularly – every six weeks?

Do you regularly attend to excess nostril, ear and neck hair? (M)

Do you regularly visit your dental hygienist?

Do you shave every morning, even on a dress-down day? (M)

You may not have considered some of these areas before, or perhaps not since those first few weeks in a new job. This next section focuses on maximizing positive impact with your grooming and ensuring that it does not get in the way of projecting your desired message.

Face Facts

As mentioned above, most of our communicating is done by the influencing triangle, of which our facial expressions and grooming are key influencing factors. So, let us focus on the face to start with.

Skincare

We know that the environment we live and work in can adversely affect the condition of our skin, and if your skin needs some help then you need to give it more attention with a regular skincare system. If you have been using the same skincare products for the past five years then it is time to try some of the new formulations that are around now. Skincare technology has moved on a long way. As women age quicker than men, you should be paying particular attention to your skin and eye area with cleansing and moisturizing products. And, guys, if you're still using soap and water to wash your face, then you're missing out on some great products now available especially for men. Good skin is an asset and bad skin will get noticed. By looking after your skin and giving it a boost you will keep it looking healthier and fresher, get rid of flaky patches and eliminate the danger of flakes of dead skin falling on to dark clothes. If you do suffer from spots and/or patchy skin, it can shift attention from your eyes and mouth and become a distraction, so it is really important to deal with them. If your skin condition does leave something to be desired, then increasing your daily intake of water, fresh fruit and vegetables will help. Stress can affect the skin condition and deplete the body of zinc, vitamin C and B vitamins, so fruit and vegetables will help. Take zinc supplements if necessary, which will also help skin to heal. If, like me, you find it difficult to eat enough fruit, then invest in a blender and make your own fruit smoothies with your choice of banana, mango, strawberries or raspberries, and mix with unsweetened orange juice – delicious! If you have dry and chapped or flaky lips, then you need to use a moisturizer to counteract it. A lip balm during the day or Vaseline at night-time are best.

Recommended Daily Skincare and Shaving Routine for Men

The skin cells regenerate every 28 days or thereabouts, but for our skin to look and feel healthy, we need to remove dead, flaky skin cells quicker than this. As you shave every day, you will be exfoliating the skin or removing these dead cells. This is what a cream exfoliator does and is why women use it, but shaving does this for you already.

A wet shave is better for getting a close shave than using an electric razor. Get the best available razor – you want to avoid hacking the skin, causing unsightly cuts and scars. Use a good-quality shaving soap that does not irritate your skin. You can get a closer shave by warming the skin with a hot towel before shaving, and by first shaving upwards, re-lathering and shaving downwards. Always apply a light moisturizer or skin balm afterwards or the skin can feel quite raw and sensitive. There are many skincare ranges just for men now – try Body Shop, Tesco or Boots. Most moisturizers now also contain sunscreens, which are essential for protecting your skin in today's environment. Never use aftershave on the shaved area directly after shaving as this dries the skin and stings like mad.

Recommended Daily Skincare Routine for Women

Your daily routine should consist of cleanse, tone and moisturize in the mornings and cleanse, tone and nourish with night cream and eye cream at night-time. I know this sounds time-consuming but it should only take 5 minutes or less, and it is time well spent. Products do not need to cost a fortune; there are many moderately priced products around that are excellent. Visit department stores and ask for some samples to try before buying. Many women skip the toner but it is important for flushing out traces of cleanser from the pores and for refining the texture of the skin. It should not sting the skin; if yours does, then it probably has an element of alcohol in or is just too harsh for your skin. Your daytime moisturizer will protect your skin against pollution from the environment and should contain a sunscreen or SPF – most good brands do. The moisturizer will also help your skin to retain moisture by extracting moisture from the air by the use of humectants. Elizabeth Arden's 8-hour cream is wonderful. Nourishing your skin at night-time is important for replacing some of the goodness lost during the day. If you feel that your skin needs an extra boost, particularly in the winter months, then you can use one of the many face masques around, or try Clarins Beauty Flash Balm, which will give your skin a pick-me-up and can be worn under make-up.

Take extra special care of your eyes, as they are the first part of your face to show signs of ageing. The skin here is thinner than it is on the rest of the face and will lose its elasticity quicker too, causing sagging and wrinkles. You need to use special eye formulations which are suited to the type of skin around the eyes, to delay and reduce the signs of ageing. A cooling eye gel is good after a hard day's work, especially if you have spent long periods in front of a computer screen.

If your skin is in good condition, then your make-up will apply more easily and stay on better. If your skin tends to be flaky, then you need to use a gentle exfoliator or facial scrub to remove dead skin cells and smooth out the skin. If you don't do this, make-up will tend to clog.

Hair

Recent research for this book showed that men and women notice people's hair before anything else, and that greasy or unclean hair is ranked one of the biggest turn-offs in the office. There are no excuses for unclean hair and you should use a good-quality conditioning shampoo suitable for your hair type. Ask your hairdresser for advice on the products best suited to your hair because there are many designed to keep hair under control. Men, do avoid the use of too much product such as gels and creams, which can make the hair look greasy. Too much slick is not appropriate for most business situations. If you have not changed your hairstyle for more than three years, then make a point of discussing this with a hairdresser at an up-to-date salon, where you can be sure that training in new techniques is a priority, and which is not necessarily your long-term traditional barber or mobile hairdresser. I come across so many women in particular who are not happy with their hairdresser but continue to go to the same one for fear of hurting feelings! I find it amazing that this happens, and I recommend that you pay a visit to another hairdresser once a year anyway, to avoid becoming stuck in a rut with the same style or ideas. You should also get your hair cut regularly – about every six weeks. Don't allow your hair to get well past its next required cut, and keep the style as it should be rather than having a grown-out version. Make your next appointment each time you go, to make things easier.

Hair Colour

There are some good ranges of hair colour available now, which really condition the hair. I find that L'Oréal's Dia Colour is wonderful. Gone are the days when hair colour damaged the hair, instead it now creates shine and looks incredibly natural. If you feel that you are too young to be going grey, then ask your hairdresser for advice on the options. A word of warning, though, make sure you go with warm or cool shades appropriate to your natural skin tones, otherwise the colour will look unnatural. Although many hairdressers now will be able to tell whether you need warm or cool colours, having analysed your best colours (see later in the chapter) it is always best to tell them what base colour suits you best. For example, with blonde hair colour, you can have golden (warm) or ash (cool) tones, and getting it wrong will have the same effect as the wrong colours against the skin. Don't go too dark if you're naturally light, and vice versa – or you can look quite ill. There are hair colours just for men too. Do consider, though, whether you really need to take this step. Is it going to look unnatural? Remember that most women find grey hair attractive.

Hands and Nails

In business, your hands and nails are often noticed, especially in meetings. I find from my clients that not only do people generally notice nails, particularly badly bitten ones, but that men in particular often remember what both men's and women's nails look like. If you are a DIY or gardening enthusiast at the weekends, make sure your nails look professional on Monday morning. Many men as well as women now have regular manicures to keep their nails and hands in good condition. A rich hand cream is important too if your hands tend to be dry – nobody likes to feel chapped or rough hands when shaking hands and it can leave a negative impression. There are many products that claim to help strengthen nails or stop the biting, but I believe that a regular manicure helps more than anything. For a start, it is even more embarrassing to go back week after week with your nails still bitten down. Keep a nail file in your briefcase or handbag and attend to any chipped or broken areas straight away to avoid any temptation to nibble at them. I worked with a CEO recently, just prior to his company's planned flotation. His aim from the session was to ensure that he and his management team presented a good, solid image with high integrity to the many financial analysts they planned to meet and present to in the coming weeks. Unfortunately, despite a generally good image himself, his nails were badly chewed right down – not good for the CEO of a company intending to present a consistently reliable, strong and solid image of an organization worth investing in. Nervous tension was the implied message – needless to say, we had to sort this out. Close-ups of politicians' nails have been printed in the media too, implying high stress levels and worry going on behind closed doors. Once again, this is an example of a picture painting a thousand words.

For women, if all else fails, you can consider nail tips or extensions which look incredibly natural, but be aware that they are high maintenance. Generally, you should keep your nails a professional length (no longer than half a centimetre past the finger-tip). Coloured nail polish is becoming more acceptable in business, and French manicures, where the tips are whitened, provide a fashionable option too. Pale, frosty colours can look dated on the over-50s.

Creasing

Please don't ruin the effect of a good suit or shirt by wearing the jacket to travel in or believing every 'non-iron' advert on the packaging. Some shirt makes are better than others and remember that the back of your jacket will be visible, particularly when presenting. For a sharp, crisp, well-presented look, your shirts will always need the attention of an iron. Please do not wear a new shirt straight from the packet without pressing it – you'll be a laughing stock. A trouser press is a good investment, but be careful not to create vertical double creases. If you are travelling, you can hang a creased suit in a steamy bathroom for 30 minutes to revive and restore the fabric and help the creases to drop out.

Teeth and Breath

I mention these here together because bad breath can often stem from badly maintained teeth. Bad breath was a high scorer in recent research on the biggest turn-offs in the office. In a global business world where we deal with the Americans and Australians more than ever, cultures that have traditionally and generally taken greater care of their teeth than the Europeans, we must ensure that our teeth don't get us noticed for the wrong reasons. It is also good to see so many of our teenagers now accepting orthodontic braces almost as a fashion accessory. Dental cosmetic treatments are becoming more affordable than ever before, with many more options available. Red wine, caffeine and smoking will all discolour your teeth and if this affects you then whitening is certainly something you should consider. Prices for whitening start from about £250, but you should talk to your dentist or hygienist about the options available.

Do visit your hygienist regularly too, for your teeth to be thoroughly cleaned. This not only feels wonderful afterwards, but ensures that bacteria do not build up causing unpleasant breath. Always carry a breath freshener in your car or briefcase, and chewing gum can help, although a word of warning – do not chew gum in meetings or when with clients. Give yourself a 'teeth check' now and make a note on your Personal Action Plan to act if need be.

Body Odour

There are no excuses for not showering daily and wearing a clean shirt or top every day. Fresh sweat on a clean and deodorized body is rarely a problem; it is old sweat coming into contact with body heat that causes the problem we are all familiar with. Make sure you change your deodorant occasionally too – if you use the same one for too long, it can lose its effectiveness. Natural fibres in clothes will help your body breathe more easily. For example, wear pure cotton shirts rather than cotton/polyester mix ones, and prefer cotton, wool or silk socks.

Accessories

Many of the messages you portray about your Personal Brand Values and the standards you have for yourself are displayed through the details of your image, such as the watch you wear or the pen you use. The way you finish off an outfit is essential to getting across your desired messages of quality and professionalism. All too often a powerful image is spoilt by bringing out a chewed old biro in an important meeting. Every self-respecting businessman or woman should own a quality pen and pencil, and a fountain pen is even more impressive. Signing your letters with a fountain pen will make a positive impact and will not go unnoticed.

Watches

I have lost count of how many times I've seen a stylish look diminished by a watch that does everything from altitude measurement to deep-sea diving! Your chunky, flashy, diamond-encrusted Rolex is also not appropriate for business. There is no better business jewellery investment than a high quality, classic-styled watch. Take a look at the options – design, colour of metal, how numbers are displayed, the weight and the size. Make sure it is right for your personality and your frame. Prices vary considerably, so there is no excuse for every businessman or woman not to own a design that will speak volumes about his/her professionalism. Buy the best you can afford – it will serve you well. Some moderately priced ranges include Rotary, Tissot, Accurist and Seiko. For real impact that will get noticed, you should aspire to some of the costliest and highest quality – Raymond Weil, Ebel, Maurice Lacroix, Cartier, Baume Mercier, Patek Philippe and Jaeger Le Coultre. *Tip*: Not wearing a watch casts doubt over your time-management effectiveness!

Briefcases, Handbags and Luggage

Your baggage is all part of your image, so you need to make sure it is portraying the same level of professionalism as the rest of your personal package. It is part of your package and is a visible accessory as soon as you arrive for an important meeting. It is just not good enough to use the same briefcase year after year until it literally falls apart. Choose one that reflects your job role and that is suitable for the normal amount of stuff you carry around. They vary in cost and quality, so go for the best quality you can afford. Black or tan are the best choices for men, with simple brass clasps. If you don't need a briefcase for a specific meeting, use a quality leather folder instead. If you regularly carry loads home with you on the train, it is worth using a backpack instead – this is much easier on the back and shoulders. But it is not too cool to arrive at an important meeting with one!

For women, there are lots of options for softer-style cases now, some with double handles that allow easier access than the hard-cased ones. Combine the contents of your handbag, and umbrella if needed, with your briefcase, to avoid looking cluttered.

Men, do try not to arrive at a meeting too cluttered with briefcase, laptop, mobile phone and Palm pilot in your pockets, umbrella, newspaper under your arm . . . you get the picture. You'll look out of control and you do need a hand easily free for the handshake. Your laptop should have its own case, so this too should reflect your image. If the one that comes with the machine is not good enough, change it.

If travelling overnight, you should also consider your luggage. There are lots of quality designs around, including Louis Vuitton, Burberry and Mulberry – put them on your Christmas list! Marks & Spencer do a great quality range too, as do Tumi. Make sure you're not the one sad person who picks up the battered old 1970s-style plastic suitcase with the rubber straps holding it together from the baggage claim carousel!

Looking the Business – Men

Dress Sense

Sorry to disappoint, guys, but I am afraid there are no magic formulae here – I am not going to give you a foolproof list of what ties to wear with what shirts and suits, and so on. In other words, I'm not going to attempt to clone you into the 'typical businessman' – your own individuality is important. However, I will be giving you guidelines that you can apply and adapt to work with your personality and PBVs to develop your own successful image. Read and use this section to help you to think 'outside the boxes' and try something different that may be more flattering and have more impact. For example, if you have always worn white shirts and double-breasted suits, then have a change – an alternative may give you more of a positive business image. Improving your dress sense and style is not something that will or should happen overnight. Too radical a change too quickly can label you inconsistent and false, so make changes gradually.

Suit Yourself

Although a suit is no longer essential for all business situations, it will still be required for your most professional look. Be careful not to get so swept up in a dress-down culture that you overlook the occasions when a suit is required and should be worn. When choosing a suit, it is important to consider your desired overall look. Is it classic British, modern, fashionable or continental? If you travel to Europe a lot on business, then you may want to portray a more global look than one of the archetypal English gent, or if your main priority is to portray creativity and flair, then a more fashionable look is for you. Be aware of your corporate culture and image as well as your intended effect and choose clothes and styles appropriately.

Many men are not aware of their best suit style. It is not just a matter of fashion and trends, but more a matter of what *suits* you too. Finding the right style, which best complements the body shape, scale and proportions, is important if you are to look well dressed, stylish and balanced. Nobody is perfect, but we don't have to walk around naked – finding the right style will hide the flaws and emphasize the good bits. Dressing for your body type is one of the most important aspects of being well dressed, and this chapter will help you to establish that. There are many different options to choose from, with varying styles, fabrics and prices. With some ideas of what is best for you, pay a visit to a large branch of a reputable menswear retailer, such as Austin Reed, Marks & Spencer or Ciro Citterio, and try a few of the options. Austin Reed, for example, stocks many designs and styles – from Hugo Boss to Chester Barrie – so this provides a haven for trying different styles and trends. In the typical high-street store you will find mixing and matching of various features of a suit to reflect current trends.

So, let's determine which style is right for you.

Consider the basics first:

- Your body shape, proportions, size, height and any figure challenges you may have (that is, short legs, paunch, broad shoulders, and so on).
- Your personality: what you like – classic, fashionable or making a statement.
- Budget – make sure this is realistic for the job that you do. It may need reassessing upwards, particularly for senior management.
- The effect – more relaxed or slick and sharp.
- Durability – how many suits are you going to need and how often are you going to rotate each one? Do you travel around a lot in a suit or spend most of your time in the office?
- Fabric weight – the season you are buying for.

Make a list from the points above to outline your particular needs.

The following styles describe four basic designs, for you to establish which elements are right for you.

The Classic 'British' Style

Neat in style and most often two- or three-buttoned single-breasted, with small, notched lapels, a nipped-in waist, and double vent or a centre vent.

European Style

This style is most often double-breasted, boxy and low buttoning, with four or six buttons. It has large and pointed lapels and is often ventless, with no shape at the waist.

Italian Style

More modern styling for a double-breasted suit, in that it has more shape at the waist, and slightly higher buttoning and pointed lapels, although the style is more subtle than the European. Can also be single-breasted and single or double vented.

Relaxed Style

This is sometimes referred to as the 'American' suit or continental style. It is great for a slightly more relaxed look because it is broader across the shoulders and the armholes are deeper. It is not often found as a formal suit but more often as a sports jacket. Be careful with this design if you have bad posture as it can make the shoulders more rounded. It is usually ventless, so this style is not good if you have a wide backside.

Suiting Fabrics

Again, there are many fabrics to choose from and this huge choice gives you the opportunity to display individualism in your suit collection. If you have not paid much attention before to the various types of fabrics and patterns around, now is your chance to think outside the boxes and consider something different that you feel and look good in. Today's fabrics are lighter than ever before, and are therefore much more comfortable to wear. Wool or worsted wool (closely woven wool yarns) remain the most popular choices. Worsted holds its shape and trouser creases well, and today Lycra is often added to wool fabric to make it more forgiving in terms of maintenance. Remember that a suit is only as good as its fabric, so it is important to make sure that the fabric you choose is going to wear well and retain its shape. Check that the fabric is either 100 per cent wool or certainly mostly wool, and it is worth noting that although wool implies warmth, light 8–9 oz weight or Super 100 worsteds will breathe well and provide the light, airy quality you need in summer. You could even get through the summer virtually crease-free. The higher the proportion of artificial fibres added, the less comfortable the fabric will be to wear in warm weather. When you select a suit, test the fabric – screw up the sleeve for a couple of seconds in your hand and make sure the fabric springs back without creasing. Don't be afraid to do this – if a shop is selling quality suits, then it won't mind you doing this – believe me, I've checked! Make sure you like the feel of the fabric too. Also, pull the fabric on the bias slightly and again make sure it regains its shape immediately. If it does not, then after a few wearings and dry-cleans the suit will lose shape and become sloppy. Beware of off-the-peg designer labels – I've seen inferior-quality fabric on these too.

Textures and Patterns

Without patterns and textures, clothes would be boring, but too many patterns going on together is too distracting, so you need to limit your outfit to a maximum of two patterns. For example, a bird's-eye weave suit, plain shirt and geometric-patterned tie. Generally try to avoid wearing two similar patterns – for example, a pinstripe suit and striped tie: this will work better if the stripe spacing on the tie and suit is different. If in doubt, opt for a different pattern in the tie. Always check the pattern matches on a jacket – for example, do the pinstripes line up at critical points such as the pockets and seams?

Look for some of these popular patterns:

- *Herringbone* – twill weave with threads running alternately to left and right to form an inverted-V design that looks like the bones of a fish. Great design for both suits and sports jackets.
- *Bird's Eye* – a tightly woven fabric with a fine diagonal diamond-shaped design. It has the appearance of small dots and is very popular for suits.
- *Glen Check* – most often a black and white distinct plaid or check. Similar to a Prince of Wales check but more subtle.
- *Nailhead or Pinhead* – a design of small dots in a straight up-and-down pattern.
- *Windowpane* – large box check formed by vertical and horizontal stripes.

What's the Difference Between a Pinstripe and a Chalk Stripe?

A question I am often asked. So, to clarify in simple terms: a pinstripe is a fine or broken (beaded) thin line with a spacing of ½cm to 4cm. A chalk stripe is wider, in fact resembling a chalked line, so is a slightly softer stripe, often set 4 cm apart. Stripes are great for a sharp business look for most environments. Traditionally they were expected in the City and, although we still see an abundance there, they are becoming an option in all types of business and you can always wear them to see the bank manager too! Because of the wonderful choices of subtle colours of stripes and the chance to match these with a brightly coloured lining (especially in made-to-measure suits), you can bring out your individualism even more. But be aware that chalk stripes are still considered very British.

For uniqueness and individuality, you could try stepping up your budget to a suit designed just for you. Those available are:

- *Bespoke tailoring* – a design measured and made specifically for you, including fabric, lining and details of style.

- *Made to measure* – made for you from a set of standard designs, but to your measurements.

Key Fabric Tips

- Choose a fabric of an appropriate weight for the environment you work in.

- Lightweight wools and worsteds travel well and do not crease so easily in warm climates.

- Test the quality of a fabric to make sure it will retain its shape.

- Don't mix more than two patterns when putting an outfit together.

- A good suit wardrobe will consist of varying fabrics, weights and patterns to suit all situations and environments.

- Be seasonal with your suits and don't wear the same ones throughout the year.

Suits You, Sir!

If you're Mr 42R you have a lot of choice with your suits, and the only considerations will be price, fabric and personal taste. If you have a few challenges with your body shape, then you will need to consider a few other elements when choosing your suits. Do remember, though, that, whatever your size or proportions, forget the size of the suit, and concentrate on good fit.

Tall, Straight and Narrow

- Avoid narrow pinstripes, as these will accentuate your narrow body.

- You can look like a beanpole in single-breasted suits.

- Go for some texture in the fabric – for example, herringbone or twill.

- Higher buttoning in the jacket will ensure that you look in proportion. Try the Italian double-breasted style with shape at the waist.

- Avoid the boxy European style of double-breasted jacket because the buttoning tends to be low and the non-waisted style will accentuate your straight up-and-down body shape.

- Closely woven rather than softer fabrics will make the most of your lean shape.

Broad, Athletic Build

- Keep your suit fabrics closely woven and crisp to accentuate your sharp build.

- Avoid the continental style of jackets with wider shoulders – these will give the illusion of rounded shoulders.

- Italian double-breasted or single-breasted styles are generally best.

- Your lapels should not be too pronounced, as this will widen the shoulders, making you look out of proportion.

Portly with Figure Challenges

- Avoid double-breasted jackets because the detail of buttons on the midriff area accentuates the areas you would probably rather diminish. Double-breasted will also make you look wider than you are.

- Opt for single-breasted designs that will make you look taller and leaner.

- Go for a single or double vent in the jacket, which will lie better on broad backsides.

- You need good crease retention in the fabrics you choose. Wool worsteds are best.

- Chalk stripes can make you appear taller and slimmer.

Small and Short

- Single-breasted styles are better on you because double-breasted suits will often swamp your fine frame.

- Pay attention to the length of the jacket – it should finish just under the curve of the backside. Any lower and you will appear shorter.

- Avoid turn-ups in your trousers because these 'shorten' the legs.

- Do not go for pronounced lapels – you will be in danger of looking comical.

- Pinstripes can add height.

Sloping Shoulders

- Always opt for jackets with padded shoulders which extend 1–2 cm off the shoulder.

- Avoid the relaxed American or continental styles because the shoulders tend to be more rounded and softer.

Long-waisted or Short-waisted?

You may already know whether you are long or short in the body – in other words, long- or short-waisted. If not, take a look at yourself in the mirror in your underwear, and decide whether your body is long or short compared with your legs. If you are long-waisted you need to avoid low buttoning in jackets – for example, the European-style double-breasted suit or two-buttoned single-breasted suit. This will draw the eye downwards and give the illusion of the body being longer and the legs shorter – particularly bad if you're short too. Three- or four-buttoned single-breasted or Italian-style double-breasted styles are better for you. If you're short-waisted, then you can afford to go with lower buttoning, such as the two-buttoned single-breasted or European-style double-breasted.

The Navy Suit v the Grey Suit

While every businessman should own a sharp navy-blue suit, there should always be a more approachable grey one in the wardrobe too.

Navy will project authority whereas grey will render you more approachable on days when it is needed, perhaps for a discussion meeting with clients or a sensitive meeting with an employee. Keep the grey tones medium to charcoal in depth, as light grey suits will never look expensive. One of my clients a couple of years ago was a young and dynamic sales executive. He came to see me six months after being promoted to sales manager in charge of a team of 10 sales executives. One of his major concerns was not lack of sales success or indeed management and motivational skills, but it was being the last to hear about a problem in the team or any issues other than those that were related to sales or clients, despite being a friendly and open sort of guy. In our session we covered a number of areas that helped him, but one aspect which stands out for him because of the impact it had on his team was the suggestion that he occasionally swap his slightly intimidating dark navy suit for a more friendly medium-grey creation a couple of days a week when in the office. He found this a really subtle way of 'softening' his image on occasions, and his team opened up more to him. So, if you are a 'navy suit' man, give this advice a try.

Trousers

Bear in mind that trousers with a pleated front will add bulk, so if this is not the intention, go for minimal pleating. Flat-fronted trousers are available occasionally for suits, but will look better on young, slim men. Always wear a belt in trousers with loops – you would be surprised at how many men I come across who don't and who look incredibly sloppy. If you are very large around the midriff you can consider braces. These can be worn with self-supporting or side-adjusting trousers with no loops, and never wear braces and a belt together. Most men will wear out the trousers to a suit well before the jacket, or they become shiny, so it is always advisable to buy two pairs of trousers wherever possible. Some shops such as Austin Reed and Marks & Spencer provide a select range, which allows you to do this and also to mix and match jacket and trouser sizes, if you are not standard suit proportions.

Blazers

While I recommend that you do have a blazer in your wardrobe, as it is the accepted dress code at corporate events such as Henley Regatta, I have to also add that it now looks dated and conservative in business environments. Use it only for events that require this type of dress and where you feel comfortable presenting a classic British look. There are lots of alternative sports jackets that are more up to date.

Care of Your Suit

There is little point in investing in good-quality suits if you don't take good care of them, because if they are abused, they will soon begin to look like they've seen better days, irrespective of price. To make sure that you don't diminish your positive image, having taken the time and effort to get the style right, take a look at my tips for good maintenance:

- Rotate your suits – they should be left to hang for at least three days before wearing again.
- Hang outside the wardrobe overnight before storing them inside to let them regain their shape.
- At least three times a year hang your suits outside to get fresh air into them, or hang them in a steamy bathroom for 30 minutes. This will help to rejuvenate the suit.
- Don't overdo the dry-cleaning – the harsh chemicals knock the guts out of fabrics and your suits will lose their shape quicker.
- Don't overload pockets – they will soon droop and the suit will look sloppy. Always take items out of pockets overnight.

- Always hang on wooden hangers and avoid metal hangers at all costs; they will serve only to damage the shape of your suits.

Shirts

Does your shirt let you down when you take your jacket off? You will not do your suit justice with shirts that are past their best or badly creased. When you buy a new suit it is always a good idea to choose some refreshing new shirts to go with it – often designers will have a range of shirts that are designed to go with the style of the suit. Investing in good-quality cotton shirts will make all the difference to a sharp business look. The best-quality shirts have a seam at the centre of the yoke (the bit that goes across the shoulders at the back) to allow more ease of movement. Do check for the quality of top-stitching and stitching of buttons too. Even if you are wearing your shirt without a tie, the look of quality is essential – some recommended shirt retailers are listed at the back of the book. Collars can soon lose their shape and bend at the corners, so buying shirts with removable collar stiffeners will help to retain the shape. Always have spare stiffeners to replace those lost in the tumble dryer – I speak from experience! – or ideally take them out before washing. A good spray starch will help to put the crispness back in shirts and collars that have been washed a few times. When your shirt collars start to fray or generally get beyond help, ditch them. You cannot afford to jeopardize your image with a distraction like this so close to the face. A double cuff and cufflinks are still considered the ultimate in men's business style, and the cuff should extend from 1 cm to 4 cm beyond the jacket sleeve, depending on personal preference. Cufflinks worn with single cuffs just look second best and cheap. White shirts are not essential for the sharp, sartorial style that you strive for – a dash of colour and pattern portrays creativity and flair. Consider some of the many striped and checked designs around now, and go for some subtle colours in your shirts. A word on short-sleeved shirts – they are never as professional as long-sleeved shirts. You can even fold up the long sleeves to just below the elbow and still look professional. I always remember one of my Italian delegates saying that in her country 'only bus drivers wear white shirts with short sleeves', and we are all familiar with the formidable Italian sense of style and elegance. And please, never wear short-sleeved shirts with a tie – you'll look ineffectual and school-boyish!

Collars

Most men can wear the traditional-cut collars or button-down, although button-down collars are more relaxed and are usually made from softer fabrics such as Oxford cloth. They rarely look sharp when worn with a tie. The hidden button-down collars (button underneath the collar tip) can be good for keeping the tips of the collar straight, but make sure they lay flat and do not crinkle. If you don't have a standard-sized neck, then you need to consider the best style of collar for you. If your neck is wide and short, then you will be better in a traditional or narrow-spread collar, and avoid the widespread collars which will accentuate the thickness of the neck. If you have a long, thin neck, then the widespread collars are better for you – narrow-spread and pointed collars will only emphasize the narrowness of your neck. Make sure your collar is comfortable without being too loose – you will look like you're wasting away if it is! At the other extreme, avoid collars that are tight enough to cause excess chubbiness to spill over the top.

To get exactly what you want from a shirt, then consider having your shirts custom-made. If you have extra-long arms or a very wide neck, you do not always get the choice you would like from the high-street stores. Prices for custom-made shirts do vary but possibly start lower than you think – the investment will be very worth while.

Ties

Oscar Wilde once said, 'A well-tied tie is the first serious step in life'. Your tie is a great way of bringing out your personality, so make sure *you* buy your own. This does not mean that because you have a great sense of humour you can wear your favourite Austin Powers number though! Recent research for this book shows that most business people consider a man who wears a motif tie to be attention-seeking or an idiot, and only 18 per cent equate it with a sense of humour – so don't always believe what your colleagues tell you. A man's tie says a lot about him, his character, his sense of style and his quality standards, so make sure that *you* choose what you wear around your neck and that it is not somebody else's choice. While your choice of tie should be in keeping with your quality of suits, do make sure that you are remembered for your overall look and not your tie! Your business ties should always be silk, and you should never skimp on the quality. Good-quality ties will always have a hand-stitched loop at the base of the seam at the back, with hand stitching all the way up. You can check this by gently easing open the seam to expose the stitches. The silk is always cut on the bias to allow it to hang straight and flat. Hold a tie up from the small end and see if it hangs straight without twisting around. If it curls at all, then it is not well made so discard it. Good-quality ties are lined with muslin to provide enough bulk for a good knot. The Italians still have the best reputation for hand-made ties – it is always worth taking a look for ties if you are in Italy, even if it is during a dash through Milan airport. Your tie width and knot should be in balance with your lapel width and in proportion to your overall size. If you have narrow lapels, don't go for wide ties or large knots. A half-Windsor knot is a standard size and a full Windsor is larger and works well with widespread collars. If you need advice on the options available or the best types of knot for you, consult a wonderful little book called *The 85 Ways to Tie a*

Tie, by Thomas Fink and Yong Mao (Fink and Mao, 1999). You will be spoilt for choice. You can also ask for assistance in any good men's outfitters. The pattern of your tie should also be in proportion to your size – for example, if you are fine-framed then avoid big, bold geometrics, and if you are broad, avoid small polka dots.

If you have a stain on your tie, never attempt to clean it off with soap and water – water can set a stain. You can buy stain-remover pads for silk but it is always best to take the tie to a specialist dry-cleaner.

Shoes

You can be sure that your shoes will always get noticed – the quality, state of repair and appropriateness to your outfit will be observed by others. Your shoes are an important part of your overall package, and it is essential that you do not let them spoil the rest of your carefully thought-out look. There is no substitute for leather soles for your most professional look, and for important business meetings and engagements you should opt for nothing less. They will be worth the investment and enhance your positive business image and impact every time. Some good makes are Church's, Jones, Barkers and Cheaney. Some quality shoemakers will totally refurbish your shoes for you and, if treated and maintained well, these shoes can last many years. Do make sure that you wear appropriate shoes with your outfit. Lace-up brogues or capped shoes are the most suitable with your business suit, but some of the increasingly popular slip-on styles can be fine as long as they are not too casual. Avoid anything else for your most professional look. Black should be worn with your smartest business suits, and Oxblood or dark brown can be considered with a business-casual look. Don't do what one banker client did: when a colleague commented that it was dress-down day (he had turned up to the office in his suit and tie) he replied, 'But I'm wearing *brown* shoes!' Do make sure that you maintain your shoes well – polish when warm and use good-quality wooden shoe trees to absorb moisture and stop the leather creasing across the top. Get them soled and heeled before they have worn down completely and ask your shoe repairer to blacken around the edge of the leather soles too. Pay particular attention to the backs of the heels – these are especially noticeable when you walk up stairs.

Belts

If your trousers have loops, always wear a belt – you'll look sloppy if you don't. Your belts should always be leather, with a buckle or clasp appropriate for the outfit. A belt that would look more at home on your Levi 501s is not suitable for your suit. Keep a check on the state of your belts and when they become frayed and scrappy, use them for your gardening trousers instead. If you have expanded a tad and have to go the next notch on your belts, make sure it isn't obvious from the state of your belt-holes!

Top Coats

Your coat, while there to protect your outfits and keep you warm, is also part of your personal package. Your 'train-spotting' anorak will just not do, and nor for that matter will any coat that does not exceed the length of your jacket. Your Barbour is for country weekends and not for your smart business look.

There are several variations on styles and it comes down to personal preference and the climate you work in. The very smart and traditional wool and/or cashmere mix Crombie-style coat is useful for the colder climates and British winters. It is mid-calf-length and single breasted, and has a centre vent and sometimes a fly front or covered buttons. Its name comes from the well-respected Crombie of Aberdeen, well known for its best coat fabrics. The traditional trench coat or raincoat is another option. It is lighter weight but sometimes comes with a removable wool lining. Remember that it is only shower proof, so it will not protect your suits in a torrential downpour. Regularly treat it with a water-repellent spray, especially after dry-cleaning. Short men should avoid wearing the belt tied around the middle as this 'chops' up the body. You can instead wear the belt tied at the back.

Always wear a suit when buying a top coat to ensure adequate movement and comfort when wearing both.

Cufflinks

As I mentioned before, cufflinks on double-cuffed shirts are stylish and should be worn for your most professional look, if not all the time. If your watch bracelet is metallic, try to team up the colour (gold or silver/pewter). There is such a great selection available now that you can afford to have quite a collection to complement your different-coloured shirts and ties. Like your tie, your cufflinks say a lot about your personality – keep them stylish although we can allow some fun here. Jewellery should be minimal, subtly enhance the total look, and never be a focal point. Avoid visual piercings – it is only in fashion and the most creative of industries that this is acceptable.

Socks

Tone your socks with your shoes – that is, black shoes, black socks. If you are wearing a dark navy suit, dark navy socks will be OK too. As with ties, motif socks can label you an idiot and attention-seeking, so avoid, except at Christmas, if you must. Cotton, wool or silk socks will allow your feet to breathe much easier than polyester mixes, and will therefore be more comfortable for you and everybody else. And please, those white ones just will not do, even if all the black ones are in the wash! To avoid picking up odd socks when dressing on dark winter mornings, always buy either navy or black and not both.

What Do I Need for my Suited Business Wardrobe?

Of course, every businessman's wardrobe requirement will be different, but I can give you some minimum guidelines.

Five Suits

- To allow for reasonable rotation and change.
- These should be in varying fabrics and colours – four in darkish tones for general business wear and one in a lighter tone – for example, medium grey.
- An extra pair of trousers for your best suits.

Twelve good-quality long-sleeved shirts

- Varying light colours and patterns.

Fifteen Ties

- Varying colours and designs to complement suits and shirts.
- Update and add to your collection regularly.

Shoes

- Two pairs of black leather-soled brogues or cap-toed lace-ups.
- One pair of black slip-on or buckled shoes, for a slightly more relaxed look.

Socks

- Twenty pairs of natural fibre (wool, silk or cotton) black or navy (depending on suit colours).

Other Men's Stuff

Make-up

No, you haven't inadvertently skipped to the women's section! Make-up is something you should be aware of for diminishing minor skin imperfections, which could be distracting.

Foundation or Base Make-up

Base make-up should be considered if your skin tone is uneven or slightly blotchy, and certainly if you are presenting under bright lights or making a TV appearance. Always apply it after a moisturizer. Choose a colour close to your natural skin tone and you will give your skin a healthy and natural appearance. Ask for advice in choosing the right product. Do not try to create a tan with foundation, it will just look false – try a tinted moisturizer instead if you feel you are looking a little sallow and pale. Body Shop do one just for men, which is oil-free and lighter than the women's product.

Concealers

These will diminish the appearance of spots and blemishes and conceal dark patches around the eyes. Once you have used one you'll never be without one again. The concealer should be slightly lighter than your skin tone to be effective. They come in small tubes which can easily be kept in a pocket of your briefcase for emergencies. Yves St Laurent's Touche Éclat is great for dark patches around the eyes.

Eyebrows

Dark and bushy eyebrows can look intimidating if they are too thick and if they meet in the middle – remember Denis Healey? Keep the area between the eyebrows clear by plucking with tweezers and, if you cannot bear to do it yourself, visit a men's grooming parlour. Most beauty salons will also provide this service for men. Electrolysis is a more permanent method of dealing with unwanted facial hair.

Beards and moustaches

Facial hair has long been considered to be a potential blight on career advancement, and this has been confirmed by the fifth annual Aziz Management Communications Index. In fact, 60 per cent of business people without beards or moustaches felt that they were a bad sign. Some thought that the person could not be bothered to shave and others felt that they were hiding something. If this translates to nearly two-thirds of your *customers* seeing you in this way, then it is a problem that needs addressing. If you must have facial hair, it is paramount in business that it is kept well groomed. There is nothing more off-putting than an overgrown appendage of facial hair, and worse still, visible leftovers from lunch! If you have had a beard or moustache for as long as you can remember, then it is time to consider whether you would look younger without it, and sharper and more appropriate for the job you now do. Get honest opinions from friends, family and colleagues. I have had several clients over the years who have told me that their family and friends prefer them without the facial hair. Beware particularly if your beard is greying – you will almost certainly look younger without it. You should also be aware that even people with perfect hearing rely on mouth movements for clarity of speech, and therefore beards and moustaches will often make communication difficult. The Aziz survey also revealed that only 7 per cent of business people associated beards with general management, so you could be in danger of damaging your promotion chances too.

Furry Ears and Nostrils

Yes, it'll hit you all after the age of 35! It is distracting and unpleasant to see, and because you are viewed more often from the side than from the front, ear hair will be noticed. You can buy special gadgets from chemists to remove unwanted ear and nostril hair and some can be used in the shower. Always attend to these areas when shaving.

Looking the Business — Women

This section is all about understanding your body shape and colouring, and working with your assets and diminishing those bits you would rather not emphasize! By understanding these elements and thinking outside the boxes a little more when buying clothes and accessories, you really can look younger, healthier and, yes, even slimmer. All of these things will make you feel good about yourself and ensure that you make a positive impact via your appearance, therefore enhancing your image.

You should remember that there are no rules for the clothes and accessories you should wear, so you will be glad to hear that this section does not include masses of checklists of what you should have in your wardrobe, as other books have done in the past. Because your clothing and grooming are seen as a reflection of the inner you, this chapter aims to provide you with enough information to open your mind to the vast array of options available now for businesswomen, and to help you to consider what is best for you and to bring out your individuality, which all combine to enhance your positive business image and impact. Although you will have a preferred style direction, maybe classic, romantic or even dramatic, try not to buy similar types of clothes all of the time. Try different stores and designers, and perhaps mix and match styles a little. For example, if you prefer a classic-styled suit or jacket, try a funky, patterned top underneath to bring out that little bit of hidden drama in you. So, the message here is be prepared to diversify and propel yourself forward with a new updated image impact.

It is better to buy quality clothes and fewer of them than lots of so-called bargains that you hardly wear. You actually probably wear only 20 per cent of your wardrobe 80 per cent of the time anyway. Something useful to remember is the 'cost-of-wearing' factor. What does a garment cost you over the course of a year, for example? A suit that cost you £300 that you wear twice a week to the office because you feel great in it costs you about £3 each time you wear it, whereas an £80 suit you wear only once a month costs you about £8 each wearing. So often cheaper, lower-quality clothes that you don't feel so good in end up costing you more.

Suit = Power?

We now live in a business world where matching suits are no longer necessary for women to create a professional image. We do not need the power suits with their heavy masculine lines that were so popular in the 1980s and early 1990s to create impact in business. We no longer need to adopt a masculine image to have personal power in all that we do, even in a male-dominated environment. If you can feel good about the way you look, then you provide yourself with the gift of added confidence, which in turn makes you feel powerful inside too. So, although a matching suit will continue to be the most appropriate option in a number of business situations, there are lots of alternatives and more deconstructed options that will also provide a professional look for you. There are many options that are suitable for the office, including edge-to-edge jackets (either open or hooked fronts), zipped fronts, collarless and military styles. Also, there is a vast choice of fabrics, and many softer and more fluid fabrics too, which are great for the curvy woman. Single-breasted jackets will look good on all women, whereas double-breasted jackets are good only on average to tall women. Your considerations when making choices for your wardrobe basics such as jackets, suits and coats are:

- Your body shape, proportions, size, height and any figure challenges you may have.
- Your personality – not trying to be somebody or something you are not.
- Budget – make sure this is realistic for the job that you do – it may need reassessing upwards.
- The effect – more relaxed or sharp and urbane.
- Versatility – can you mix and match with other items in the wardrobe?

So, let's now delve deeper than the basics and help you to understand your best choices from the myriad possibilities.

What is Right for Me?

We all have that favourite outfit in the wardrobe that makes us feel wonderful every time we wear it. Why *is* that? It is probably because we've received compliments when wearing it, and therefore it is likely to be one of our best colours and the style and fit balanced for our body shape and proportions. Many things constitute a good image, and although the criteria are the same for everybody, the specifics are very different.

Principles to Aim for

- To look balanced and appropriate.
- To be immaculate and consistent in your grooming.
- A look that reflects your personality and is not copied from someone else.
- A look that shows attention to detail.
- A look that wins you respect before you even open your mouth.

One of the first steps in choosing the right clothes is to understand your basic body shape. No matter what your body shape and proportions are, by recognizing them and by using a little bit of the art of illusion, we can all look great, increase positive impact and command respect through our appearance. You can learn to diminish the lumps and bumps and make more of the good points until it becomes a habit and therefore easier and a way of life. There are many good books illustrating the various designs and cuts of clothes suitable for different body shapes; some are listed at the back of the book and therefore my aim in this chapter is to give you my short, sharp tips with the aim of avoiding diminishing image impact through your clothes.

Style books will often describe a few different body shapes, suggesting that you can categorize women's bodies into one of six or so shapes. There are, of course, many hundreds of different shapes around, with no two women the same, so it is pointless to attempt to prescribe specific styles for a specific shape. While a pear-shaped woman has a wider bottom half, she can also be short or tall, wide or narrow, and so it makes sense to deal with the various imbalances such as wide shoulders, little waist definition, and so on, individually.

First of all, though, and most importantly, you do need to ascertain whether your body is straight or curved, or perhaps a bit of both. It's time to be honest with yourself and stand in front of the mirror in your underwear – sorry!

Tick the appropriate boxes to understand your basic body shape:

	Straight		*Curved*	
Shoulders	Straight and/or wide	☐	Narrow and/or sloping	☐
Torso	Wide and/or straight	☐	Narrow and/or shaped	☐
Waist	Little or no definition	☐	Clearly defined	☐
Hips/thighs	Straight down from waist	☐	Flared out from waist	☐

Straight Body Shape

If you have a straight body shape, then sharper, more tailored clothes will make you look and feel good. Tailored styles will emphasize your elegant lines, creating impact every time. Princess Diana looked fantastic in the straighter and more elegant styles she wore in the latter years of her life. The soft flounces of her wedding dress did nothing for her straight shape, and the frills around the neck hid her attractive angular neckline. Understanding and working with your basic bodylines are important for looking balanced, comfortable and confident.

Key Tips

- Tailored jackets with waist shaping – this will give the illusion of more waist definition.
- Angular rather than curvy lines in lapels and pockets.
- Lightly padded shoulders.
- Top stitching in jackets can be striking.
- Crisp, tightly woven fabrics in suits.
- Defined pleats and creases in trousers.
- Geometric patterns, checks and pinstripes rather than swirly, soft foulards.
- Straight rather than curved hemlines.
- Not too much texture in fabrics.

Curvy Body Shape

Curvy body lines are incredibly feminine, and the only danger is over-emphasizing this to a point where you lose credibility in the workplace. There are many softer designs of suits available for businesswomen now that still retain the right level of smartness.

Key Tips

- Soft tailoring.

- Deconstructed designs such as edge-to-edge and collarless jackets.

- Softly woven fabrics.

- Jackets should lie flat against the curves of the body.

- Fabric should drape well.

- Rounded shoulders should be corrected with light shoulder padding.

- Belted jackets and belts to emphasize waist definition.

- Curvier lapels rather than pointed ones.

- Stripes and checks can look unbalanced on a curvy body.

Camouflaging the Figure Challenges

Very few women have perfect bodies, but we can use clothing to cover up and diminish our imperfections. As I mentioned earlier, knowing a little about the art of illusion helps when it comes to hiding the bits we are not keen on. Your overall aim is to attract the onlooker up towards your face, and you need a silhouette that enhances this.

Broad Shoulders

Go for:	*Avoid:*
Light or no shoulder padding. Good fit on the shoulders for tops and jackets and do not extend past them. V-necks or scooped round necks.	Heavy padding on shoulders that widen. Epaulettes. Cap sleeves. Wide or slash necklines. Wide lapels.

Narrow or Sloping Shoulders

Go for:

Shoulder pads – you can buy removable ones too.

Slash necklines which widen the shoulders.

Cap sleeves.

Details on the shoulders.

Brooches positioned wide which draw the eye outwards.

Horizontal stripes in tops.

Avoid:

V-necks as these narrow the shoulders.

Very narrow lapels.

Fine vertical striped tops.

Knitwear with low shoulder seams.

Long or Thin Necks

Go for:

Scarves at the neckline.

High neck jackets such as Mandarin collar.

Polo and turtlenecks.

Choker-style necklaces.

Fill open necks with jewellery.

Avoid:

Severe V-necks.

Shirt buttoned low.

Scarves that tie low down.

Short Neck

Go for:

Lower necklines such as scoop or V-neck.

Open collars.

Long pendant necklaces.

Collarless jackets.

Avoid:

Scarves tied high.

Choker-style necklaces.

Polo and turtlenecks.

Mandarin collars.

Small Bust

Go for:

Layering on the top half of the body.

Horizontal lines in tops to add width.

Texture to add bulk.

Breast pockets.

Padded and cleavage-enhancing bras.

Avoid:

Vertical stripes on top half of body.

Tightly fitting tops – for example, Lycra.

Large Bust

Go for:

Plain and matt fabrics on top half of body.

Round- or scoop-necked tops.

V-necked tops if not too low cut.

Vertical or diagonal patterns on tops.

Collarless jackets.

Avoid:

Shiny fabrics on top.

Breast pockets.

Brooches on lapels.

Tightly fitting tops.

Horizontal patterns.

Texture in tops.

Layering.

Heavy patterns.

Large Hips and Bottom or Pear Shape

Go for:

Shoulder padding to balance out the body.

Jewellery and scarves to draw attention to the top half.

Plain and matt fabrics on bottom half.

Avoid:

Texture and patterns on bottom half.

Gathers in skirts and trousers.

Flap pockets on jackets and trousers.

Dark colours on bottom half help to diminish.

Wear patterns on top half (if not large busted).

Slashed pockets.

Longer-style jackets, finishing below the hips (or thighs if these are wide too).

Tightly fitting trousers and skirts showing VPL.

Jackets and tops finishing on the hips – emphasizing the widest point.

Light colours in trousers and skirts unless a suit.

Wide legs

Go for:

Longer-style skirts or trousers.

Shoes open across the foot – that is, court shoes.

Dark and matt hosiery.

Avoid:

Skirts finishing at widest point of calf.

Shiny hosiery.

Strappy shoes and sandals.

Proportions – Long-waisted or Short-waisted?

Most of us are either longer or shorter in the body – that is long- or short-waisted. So visit the mirror again and take a look at your proportions. Here are my tips for correcting any imbalance:

Short-waisted

Go for:

Thin belts the same colour as the top half to elongate the body.

Avoid:

Wide belts.

Patterns and textures on top half.

Single-buttoned, edge-to-edge or lower-buttoning jackets.

Uplifting bra to maximize space between bust and waist.

Plain colours on top half.

Tops and blouses worn outside of trousers (if garment style is designed for this).

High-waisted trousers and skirts with tops tucked in.

High-buttoning jackets.

Long-waisted

Go for:

Wider belts the same colour as bottom half.

Short tops or tops tucked in.

Higher buttoning on jackets.

High-waisted styles.

Patterned tops.

Toned skirt/trousers and hosiery/shoes to elongate legs.

Avoid:

Patterned trousers and skirts combined with plain tops.

Very thin belts.

Low-waisted trouser styles.

Petite Figure

I can empathize with this category as I fall into it myself. In business it can present a challenge and we have to work harder at making an impact, not having the physical stature to help us. A few simple guidelines, however, can make all the difference. As a general rule, keep your accessories, patterns and textures in scale with your body frame, and remember that tailored, neat styles will flatter most.

Tips for Looking a Few Inches Taller

- Suits work best because toning the colour all the way through in jacket, skirt/trousers/dress and shoes/boots will maintain height.

- Avoid turn-ups in trousers which just serve to 'chop' the leg off short!

- Keep attention up high – that is, in the top half of the body and in the face.

- Avoid long skirts – shorter, neater styles are best.

- Tapered or straight trousers with vertical creases elongate the legs.

- Keep the silhouette as slim as possible, avoiding gathers and fullness.

- Short, neat hairstyles help too.

- Vertical patterns elongate the body.

- Avoid scarves tying low as this will draw the eye downwards.

- Keep the foot clear of straps and wear court-style shoes with skirts.

- Avoid clumpy shoes.

- Avoid too much texture in fabrics.

- Keep accessories in scale – avoid large, heavy designs.

The Fuller Figure

Being moderately overweight does not necessarily have a negative impact in business as long as you know how to dress for best effect. In fact, it can be an asset for women as it immediately gives presence and impact, especially if you have the height to balance the body out. I have some very simple guidelines to dressing for fuller figures and there are many books written on the subject too.

My Top Tips

- Choose softer, fluid fabrics that drape the body well. Although some tailored suits are available for very curvy body shapes, they are rarely flattering.

- Darker tones will always be slimming and more flattering.

- Keep attention to the face by good use of accessories and colour.

- Make sure your clothes are never tight – you'll look a size bigger.

- Get your underwear properly fitted. Make use of the many body-control under-garments available.

- Avoid high necklines and choker-style necklaces.

- Keep your accessories in proportion to your body scale and go for large and slightly dramatic designs.

- Avoid shiny fabrics and hosiery.

- Avoid gathers and pleats.

- Choose substantial heels on shoes and avoid narrow heels.

Other Options for Business

Jersey and Knitwear

Fine knitted or jersey jackets, dresses and cardigans are good alternatives to a tailored jacket in the office, and twin sets and cardigans can look great with tailored trousers or skirts. Jersey is also wonderfully flattering for the fuller figure. Avoid chunky knits and go only for good-quality wool, cotton and silk mixes to retain professionalism and business impact. Avoid heavily patterned knits – plain colours finished off with accessories are best. Adhere to the cleaning instructions, which will usually be hand wash or dry clean, and use gentle washing detergents.

Dresses

I mean tailored dresses and not sundresses. Keep the fabric plain and neutral coloured generally and finish off with a suitable jacket or cardigan. Shift dresses provide a versatile addition to the wardrobe, and look elegant with a scarf at the neck.

Shoes

It has to be said that most people will notice other people's shoes – you're probably as guilty. But how much attention do you pay to yours and do they let you down? Some working women buy a couple of inexpensive pairs for the office and wear them to death, then throw them away and buy new ones. Cheap designs are obvious and tend to look cheap, even after two or three wears. Cheap shoes should be avoided if you are serious about improving your image impact. Shoes also can date quickly in cut and heel shape so do a shoe audit every six months and replenish your collection if need be. I know that you won't need any excuse to buy shoes, but do have a good basic collection of four or five pairs in neutral colours and classic styles. Shoes are a good way of showing that you are aware of fashion too. Small details that reflect current trends are useful, although of course they may date quicker. Good-quality shoes are worth looking after – polish them when warm, if you can bear it after a hard day's work, and use wooden shoe trees to absorb moisture and stretch out the leather to keep the tops from creasing. Get them heeled and soled before they wear down completely. It is important that you keep a pair in the car for driving in because heels quickly become scuffed. This will always be visible to others, particularly if you're walking up the stairs or are on a stage, presenting. A small to medium heel will always be the most professional, although flatter, loafer styles are great with trousers for a more relaxed look. Boots are also now acceptable with trousers.

In terms of colour, your shoes should never be lighter than your hemline. Always try to tone your hosiery with your shoes and skirt/trousers rather than making that awful mistake of black skirt, light tights and black shoes! Yes, I know some uniforms require it . . . ummm? Open-toed sandals are never professional, and sling-backs are a better alternative for business in the summer. Strappy shoes should be kept for the weekends.

Accessories – the Finishing Touches

They may seem incidental, but the role of accessories in finishing a look or an outfit is essential to gaining the right impact. Believe me, over the past few years I have seen many a potentially wonderful look destroyed by lack of, unsuitable, inappropriate or cheap accessories. The accessory market has exploded in recent months and gives us vast choices of jewellery, handbags, belts, scarves and hair accessories. Getting it right shows attention to detail and careful thought, which can be considered a reflection of your approach to business. Do be careful with matching accessories – nowadays they look contrived and show lack of flair, so keep them for weddings! Remember, it is not enough to follow the guidelines for dress styles and body shapes alone; you have to go that extra step to command respect and create real impact with your personal presentation.

Jewellery

The past few years have seen a minimalistic approach to jewellery after the often-dramatic styles of the 1980s and 1990s. However, we are now moving towards a culture that uses accessories, particularly jewellery, to reflect personality and therefore to express our individuality, which we have already seen is so powerful for our image impact. If your jewellery drawer is looking particularly depleted or dated, then take this as a nudge to update and add to it. Your jewellery should be as up-to-date as your suits. You don't need to have masses of choices, just a few well-chosen, good-quality pieces that you have selected yourself. Although jewellery always makes a nice present, it rarely reflects your choice and personality if it's bought for you. I meet lots of women who say that they don't wear jewellery and, admittedly, jewellery is not something we tend to go out and buy for ourselves. A few years ago, however, I came across a wonderful range for businesswomen, in terms of high quality, choice and comfort, called Pierre Lang (for contact details, see the back of the book), which you can see and try on at home, making life easier. I love the stuff! If you don't like jewellery to stand out, then opt for the matt silver and gold finishes now available, which are fashionable yet more discreet.

Your jewellery should not only reflect personality, but body scale too. You do not want to look ridiculous with lots of heavy jewellery if you have a fine-framed figure, and delicate pieces on a fuller frame look equally odd – this is a common mistake. Brooches too can be a wonderful addition to your collection, but don't overdo it with necklace, brooch *and* earrings. In fact, be careful not to over-accessorize. I recommend you use a points system – count one point for every piece of jewellery you wear at the same time. If you reach 10, then you are overdoing it. One necklace at a time and no more than two pairs of earrings, please. Too much jewellery and you will create a negative distraction. Nose and tongue piercings are not professional by any stretch, with perhaps the exception of a high fashion environment and/ or industry. Do try to vary the jewellery that you wear from day to day, and outfit to outfit too. Bracelets can be a noisy distraction in a meeting – generally avoid them for business.

Cufflinks for women make a bit of a statement and look great on a crisp cotton shirt. Traditional men's outfitters T. W. Lewin now have a section just for women.

Belts

Although belts are a wonderful accessory to have in the wardrobe, a word of warning is required. Matching belts with shoes is today an easy way to look like you are stuck in a 1980s time warp. Instead, be aware of what is in fashion and choose a few good-quality designs that complement and finish your outfits well. Watch the clasps and belt around the buckle area and bin it when it becomes visibly worn.

Underwear and Hosiery

My mother always used to say, 'when you put your underwear on in the morning, make sure you'd be proud of it if you got knocked down by a bus'! Bizarrely, this has stayed with me, and when I sort out my underwear drawer a couple of times a year I always have this in mind. You can feel a like million dollars in good-quality and well-fitted underwear. So, rule number 1 – get your bras properly fitted. It is an all-too-common occurrence to see unsightly bulges oozing out of an ill-fitting bra, back and front. The most common mistakes women make are choosing a cup size too small and a chest size too big. If the chest size is too big, the back of the bra is often worn too high to give support, and this then results in a very obvious bad-fitting bra under clothes. The front and the back of a bra should be level – that is, the same height – and not higher at the back. Always try to tone your underwear to your clothes – it should not be visible in a working environment. Flesh-coloured underwear is less visible under white than white underwear, so it is always good to have a set in the drawer.

Do not fall foul of VPL (visible panty line) – this is caused by underwear or clothes being too tight. G-strings are marvellous for avoiding this problem and there are some really comfortable designs around now. Body smoothers for the excess lumps and bumps, and waist clinches for extra waist definition, are a godsend. Nancy Ganz bodies and Barbara of Paris corsets are particularly effective.

Tights or stockings should be worn at all times when wearing a skirt in the office – bare legs are never professional. In the heat of the summer, wear fine denier stockings for comfort. Do ditch hosiery when it becomes snagged or keep it for under trousers only – yes, I do that too! The most expensive brands are not always the ones that last the longest and, with careful washing, you can keep your hosiery in good condition for longer. Your hosiery should be toned to your shoes and clothes where possible. Having said that, if you're still wearing navy tights then you already scored a negative on the dated image questionnaire. Pewter, charcoal or vaguely black are suitable alternatives.

Grooming Specifics

Facial Hair and Moles

These do need attention as they can be incredibly distracting. We all have hairs on our faces naturally, but if you have dark hair then a noticeable moustache effect can occur. This can be treated with either electrolysis, which provides a permanent solution, or bleaching. If you have any particularly large or unsightly moles then seek professional advice for possible treatments, including removing hair from around the mole.

Make-up

I know, I know, you're a busy businesswomen and mother and don't have time for make-up in the mornings. However, it is a fact that women who wear make-up in business generally get better jobs, get promoted quicker and get paid more. Has that got your attention? Whether we like it or not, we do live in a very visual world and we get judged on appearances. In fact, in the fifth annual Aziz Management Communications Index, in companies with an annual turnover exceeding £30 million, 64 per cent of directors believe that women wearing make-up look more professional, and 18 per cent of directors say that women who do not wear make-up 'look like they can't be bothered to make an effort'. Furthermore, 11 per cent even say that they are more likely to employ a woman who wears make-up rather than one who does not. This is not necessarily politically correct, I know, but it is an important fact and make-up will help increase the power and influence you have.

Most of us love to see a perfectly made-up face, but many women still wear little if any make-up for business or stick to the same colours and techniques as they have done for the past 10 years. Having done many makeovers for private clients and for TV, I can say that it is always the make-up that makes the most difference. Wonderful clothes and a new hair-do are never enough if the face is bland. So, you see, you could be losing impact which will take you only 10 minutes in the morning to regain. I have provided my top tips below, but I also recommend visiting an image consultant or beauty therapist for a make-up lesson if you are stuck in a rut with your make-up. Take along your make-up bag and revamp it. Make-up does have a shelf life, so if you have products that have been there for years, then bin them and replenish.

A Long-lasting Business Make-up

By following these tips, your make-up should last you all day at the office. You may only need to touch up with powder and replenish your lipstick.

- A make-up base really helps your foundation to last all day (try Sisley or Boots' own make). Select a foundation that matches the colour of your skin tone or is one tone darker at most. A common mistake is choosing a foundation that is too dark and looks false. The idea of foundation is to even out the skin tone and to look natural and fresh. Liquid foundations often look more natural, or try Vincent Longos' Water Canvass, which gives a very smooth effect.

- If you have dark patches around the eyes or in the corners against the nose, then using a concealer will help. Concealers need to be lighter than your foundation to give the desired results. A favourite of mine for diminishing shadows and lines is Yves St Laurent's Touche Éclat.

- If a blusher disappears on you, try using a cream blusher *before* you apply powder, then add a soft dash of powder blusher on top.

- Apply loose translucent powder to set your foundation using a powder puff or by pressing in with cotton wool. Within minutes it will be absorbed and will last longer.

- A light eye base applied all over the lid before any eye shadow helps your eye shadow last 12 hours or more without creasing or disappearing. I could not live without Color Me Beautiful's Eye Base!

- Use soft, neutral colours for your eye shadow. Apply a lighter base colour and keep darker colour to the outer lid to give depth and interest. If using eyeliner, keep it soft. Harsh lines are severe and can make the eyes look smaller. A soft line along the outer third of your top and lower eyelids, using a rich kohl pencil, makes your eyelashes look thicker.

- For eyebrows, use a soft taupe or brown eye shadow, lighter than the colour of your own eyebrows, to fill in any uneven patches (more natural-looking than using pencil).

- Apply a light lip base before using lip liner and lipstick to moisturize lips and create a base for lipstick to adhere to. It helps your lipstick stay on much longer.

- Apply lip pencil in a natural colour all over your lips before using lipstick – it also helps your lipstick last longer and avoids unsightly lines left around your lips if your lipstick wears off. *Useful tip:* to reduce the amount of lipstick sticking to your cup or glass, discreetly lick the cup before drinking – you'll notice that your lipstick stays on the lips instead!

- Touch up your powder to avoid shine and reapply lipstick a couple of times during the working day.

- Try not to touch your face excessively.

Handbag Make-up Repair Kit

There is no need to carry around your entire make-up bag, but I do suggest you carry a few essential items to help keep you looking fresh throughout the day:

- Solid powder compact for shiny areas.

- Soft kohl eye pencil.

- Lipstick and gloss for freshening up.

- Mirror.

- Tissues.

Fragrances

Your aim should be for a naturally fresh odour every day, because the way we smell is part of our total image. You should opt for a light fragrance or lightly perfumed body spray for your work environment because research shows that heavy fragrances are off-putting and can result in negative impact in meetings and interviews. Bear in mind that some people's sense of smell is more acute than others' and we have all got memories of over-powering scents in the office!

Colour for Impact

This section of my workshops and consultations is always one of the most dramatic, best remembered, and lots of fun. To actually analyse and see the marked differences between the most flattering tones and positively awful ones against the skin means that you can immediately make a visual difference to the way you come across. The colours that you wear against your face are vitally important to the impact you make and for holding attention to the face. It is therefore important that you understand which tones and depths of colours are most suited to your natural colouring. This section will provide some clear guidelines for you to ascertain your best colours. For some individual advice you can visit an image consultant for a colour analysis consultation to provide you with a full understanding of what works best for you and a complete wallet of colour swatches.

Your optimum colours are determined from your hair, skin and eye colour. You need to take into account your:

- *Depth* of colouring – whether your eyes, hair and skin tone are light, medium or strong in depth.

- *Clarity* – whether your overall colouring is bright and clear. Often the eyes will be bright blue or green, in contrast with dark hair, and the skin fresh, bright and unblemished.

- *Undertone* – the most important aspect. This is predominantly determined by your skin tone. All colours have either a yellow-base (warm tones) or a blue-base (cool tones), and some are neutral. Warm colours look best against a warm skin tone and cool colours best against a cool skin tone.

Determining Warm and Cool Undertones

I'm sure that you've had people tell you that you look well or perhaps younger or slimmer when wearing a particular colour jacket or shirt, or, on the other hand, ask you whether you're feeling OK or whether you've had a late night the night before, even when you're feeling just fine! Comments like this are often down to the undertone of colour you are wearing against the face. The good news is, even if you're feeling terrible, then wearing colours that make you look healthier and alert can fool everyone – that is, if you want to. So, how do we know what is good? Take a strong orange (warm) item or piece of fabric and a plum-toned (cool) one and put each one in turn against your face. Does the orange tone make the skin look warm and healthy or sallow and yellowy? What about the plum, does it make your skin and eyes look clearer or does it make you look washed out? If in doubt, try a mossy green (warm) and a lilac (cool) and get a second opinion. So, now you have ascertained what skin tone you have. There are also some universal colours that can be worn effectively by everybody – purple, turquoise, teal, taupe, emerald green and soft white.

Now for some 'colours-that-suit-you' suggestions.

Deep Colouring

Characteristics: Dark hair and strong dark eyes. Skin usually has strength of tone but can be quite pale too. It will often tan easily.

Overall look: strength and intensity of colouring

Key Tips

- Keep strength of colour against the face.

- Create some contrast for impact – for example, navy and white or charcoal and red.

- Can also wear two dark colours together – for example, purple and black – or men can wear tie and shirt in matching darker tones.

- Avoid icy and pale colours on their own.

Famous Deep Women: Victoria Beckham, Demi Moore, Whitney Houston.

Famous Deep Men: Pete Sampras, Antonio Banderas, Tiger Woods.

Neutral Colours (for Suits, Jackets, Trousers and Coats)

- Black – a pinstripe or contrasting stitching, a fleck or pattern in the fabric will break the severity of plain black.

- Dark brown, deep charcoal, navy, deep olive, pine green, taupe (in summer and when contrasted with a darker colour).

Suggested Accent Colours for Warm Undertone (for Shirts, Ties, Tops and Scarves)

- Tomato red, scarlet red, cinnamon, rust, mahogany, pumpkin orange, deep purple, medium blue, emerald green, olive, deep peach, yellow, turquoise.

- White can work but needs dark contrast against it.

Suggested Accent Colours for Cool Undertone

- Royal blue, scarlet red, deep purple, lilac, white, plum, mint, blue green, turquoise, fuchsia pink, icy blue, icy pink.

Colours to Avoid

- Light or pastel colours worn together.
- Medium-depth colours which can look wishy-washy – for example, charcoal blue or jade.

Light Colouring

Characteristics: Blonde hair, light skin and pale eyes.
Overall look: Fair, although skin can also tan easily.

Key Tips

- Light to medium-depth colours should be used.
- Don't overpower your colouring with very strong colours and always balance darker shades with lighter shades against the face.
- Never team dark shirts or tops with solid dark ties or jackets.

Famous Light Women: Claudia Schiffer, Gwyneth Paltrow, Cate Blanchett.
Famous Light Men: Chris Tarrant, Prince William, Paul Hogan.

Neutral Colours (for Suits, Jackets, Trousers and Coats)

- All shades of grey, medium to light navy, charcoal blue, taupe, stone, beige.

Suggested Accent Colours for Warm Undertone (for Shirts, Tops, Ties and Scarves)

- Ivory or soft white, peach, light yellow, aqua, scarlet red (not too much), medium blue, warm pink, salmon pink, medium purple, periwinkle, moss green, tan, camel.

Suggested Accent Colours for Cool Undertone

- Icy pink, lilac, pale blue, aqua, periwinkle, scarlet red (not too much), jade, mint, light teal, rose pink.

Colours to Avoid

Two dark colours together against the face.

Warm Colouring

Whereas some people have warm undertones, there are some with very dominant warm colouring. They have the following attributes:

Characteristics: Golden, red or auburn tones to the hair with warm skin tones. The skin is usually freckled. The eyes can be shades of green, brown or blue.

Overall look: Warmth.

Key Tips

- All colours worn must have a warm undertone (yellow-based).

- The neutrals should always be worn with a warm colour against the face.

- Medium-depth colours work best.

Famous Warm Women: Sarah Ferguson (Duchess of York), Geri Halliwell, Nicole Kidman.

Famous Warm Men: Mick Hucknall, Chris Evans, Boris Becker.

Neutral Colours (for Suits, Jackets, Trousers and Coats)

- All shades of brown, medium to light navy, stone, camel, olive, medium grey.

Suggested Accent Colours (for Shirts, Ties, Tops and Scarves)

- Moss green, olive, brown, orange (not always professional unless in pattern), yellow, ivory, tomato red, bronze, turquoise, deep purple, coral, salmon pink, warm pink, forest green, terracotta, rust.

Colours to Avoid

- Icy pink and icy blue, wine, burgundy, black, pure white.

Cool Colouring

Whereas some people have cool undertones, there are others with very dominant cool colouring. They are those with the following attributes:

Characteristics: Ash, grey or silvery white hair, or strong dark tones with grey flecks. Blue, green, grey or cool brown eyes, rosy skin.

Overall look: Cool and striking.

Key Tips

- Create contrast – for example, put mint green with dark grey.
- Blues and purples look great.

Famous Cool Women: Germaine Greer, Margaret Thatcher, Dame Judi Dench.

Famous Cool Men: Michael Parkinson, Richard Gere, Anthony Hopkins.

Neutral Colours (for Suits, Jackets, Trousers and Coats)

- Taupe, pewter, charcoal to light grey, navy, charcoal blue, pine green.

Suggested Accent Colours (for Shirts, Ties, Tops and Scarves)

- All blues and purples, plum, aubergine, white, bright pink, turquoise, pine green, icy colours, raspberry, teal, blue red, scarlet red.

Colours to Avoid

- Black, unless with a bright colour. It can look very sombre on Cool people.

- Yellow-based colours – the wardrobe should be devoid of warm tones, such as camel, yellow, cinnamon and orange.

Medium Depth, Muted Colouring

Characteristics: Medium-depth blonde to brown hair, light to medium-depth skin, eyes can be dark or blended colours with little definition in colouring.

Overall look: Blended, muted and balanced.

Key Tips

- Avoid sharp contrasts – for example, black and white.
- Medium-depth colours such as charcoal blue and aqua are best.
- Avoid bright colours and patterns which can overwhelm.

Famous Soft Women: Hillary Clinton, Princess Anne, Cindy Crawford.
Famous Soft Men: Jonathan Ross, Jamie Oliver, Sir Paul McCartney.

Neutral Colours (for Suits, Jackets, Trousers and Coats)

- Medium to charcoal grey, charcoal blue, navy, light navy, stone, taupe, pewter, grey green.

Suggested Accent Colours for Warm Undertone (for Shirts, Ties, Tops and Scarves)

- Soft white, cream, salmon pink, warm pink, periwinkle, medium purple, moss green, turquoise, peach, coral, camel, coffee brown.

Suggested Accent Colours for Cool Undertone

- Jade, rose pink, mint green, rose brown, teal, periwinkle, medium purple, amethyst, medium blue, turquoise, deep purple, soft white.

Colours to Avoid

- Strong contrast and very bright, solid tones.

Clear Colouring

Characteristics: Usually dark hair or dramatic colour. Bright, clear eyes, which are often blue and are in clear contrast to hair. Skin light to dark and clear.
Overall look: Fresh and clear.

Key Tips

- Create contrast with dark and light colours.

- Bright and clear colours such as bright purple look fantastic.

- Avoid medium-depth colours such as moss green as these look uninteresting on you.

Famous Clear Women: Catherine Zeta Jones, Oprah Winfrey, Liz Hurley.
Famous Clear Men: Pierce Brosnan, Donny Osmond, Andre Agassi.

Neutral Colours (for Suits, Jackets, Trousers and Coats)

- Black, dark brown, dark navy, charcoal, stone and taupe.

Suggested Accent Colours for Warm Undertone (for Shirts, Ties, Tops and Scarves)

- Bright purple, bright pink, true red, turquoise, orange, bright yellow, mango, true green, clear teal, deep rose, ivory.

Suggested Accent Colours for Cool Undertone

- Bright purple, royal blue, bright pink, plum, Chinese blue, turquoise, icy pink, icy lilac, mint, icy blue, emerald turquoise.

Colours to Avoid

- Medium-depth and dull colours, and two light colours together.

You will now have worked out which tones and depths of colours are best for you, but you should also bear in mind these rules for creating effect with colour:

- An authoritative look requires depth of colour and contrast, for example:
  - *For women*: a dark charcoal suit and periwinkle top.
  - *For men*: dark navy suit, light purple shirt and woven silk tie with purple/blue.
- An approachable look requires medium-depth colours, for example:
  - *For women*: a light navy suit with either darker or lighter top, depending on your colouring.
  - *For men*: medium grey suit with ivory shirt and grey/blue tie.

In business:

- Dark colours are authoritative.
- Medium colours are approachable.
- Light or pastel colours are ineffectual.
- Brighter accent colours add impact.

A Positive Business Image

So, you have read and absorbed a great deal of information now about the way you can package yourself and improve your appearance for greater impact. Do remember, though, that your image should keep evolving and that you should not stand still for too long. Take the view that you can always improve and enhance the way you look and that creating positive impact is a self-educational journey, not a destination. You should not aim to change your image overnight but instead over a period of a few weeks or months and you should revisit this book, particularly this section, every two months to move to the next stage of your journey. To keep you on track I have summarized my top tips for dress and grooming, and top image wreckers too (W = Women, M = Men).

Positive Impact Dressing Tips

- Never have a slob day – your appearance and grooming need to be consistent in order to maintain personal power.

- Good fit, good fit and good fit!

- Make sure you look today and not yesterday.

- Your clothes should be an extension of you – style, colour, personality, your job and lifestyle.

- Pay attention to detail – it does pay off.

Top Image Wreckers

- Badly fitting clothes.

- Dated appearance.

- Lack of make-up. (W)

- Uncared-for teeth.

- Bad breath.

- Motif ties. (M)

- Excess or unkempt facial hair.

- Ill-kempt nails.

- Body odour.

- Clothes and accessories that are past their best.

- Scuffed and unpolished shoes.

- Badly co-ordinated clothes.

- Inappropriate clothing showing too much flesh. (W)

- An abundance of floral patterns and/or pastel colours. (W)

- Snagged hosiery (W)

Wardrobe Tips

- Choose suits appropriate to your job, personality, body shape and your desired effect.

- When buying a new suit, always invest in a few co-ordinating shirts and ties, or tops too.

- De-junk your wardrobe at least every 6 months and reinvest where necessary. Buy at least one high-quality suit each autumn and spring, two for men.

- Remember that it is better to wear a suit that looks fantastic many times than something cheaper and insignificant infrequently.

- Pay attention to quality – fabric, buttons, stitching and line-up of pattern at seams and pockets.

- Ditch any clothes past their best or that look dated. Women, you can often update jackets by just changing the buttons.

- Always buy within your colour guidelines – this way your wardrobe will become more versatile and co-ordinated.

- Hang jackets on wooden hangers – they will lose their shape on metal hangers.

- Buy clothes for today's size and not tomorrow's goal weight.

- Men, always buy your own ties.

- Buying good-quality cotton shirts will make a difference. (M)

- Leather-soled shoes will be one of your best investments. (M)

- Think outside the boxes and try something different. Visit some stores or designers you have never tried before – you may be surprised.

Tips for Wardrobe Maintenance

- Always give your suits time to relax after wearing. Rotate your suits with a three-day rest in between wearing.

- Hang your suits outside in the fresh air two or three times a year.

- Polish your shoes when warm.

- Use shoe trees to keep the shape and the leather from creasing.

- Always iron shirts, even the 'non-iron' variety.

- Deal with stains straight away and seek professional help if needed.

- Keep your shirt collars stiff with collar stays. (M)

- Use a spray starch to keep your shirts crisp.

- Use a trouser press but be careful not to create double creases. (M)

- Avoid over dry-cleaning – the chemicals eventually knock the guts out of fabrics.

- Get rid of creases by hanging jackets and suits in a steamy bathroom. Useful when travelling.

- Make repairs straight away rather than leaving the item in the wardrobe until needed.

Quality Construction – What to Look For

- Seams should be clearly finished and not pull or wrinkle.

- Interfacings and facings should not wrinkle, gape or pull.

- Hemlines must hang evenly.

- Pockets must be straight and lie flat.

- Look for quality buttons.

- Buttonholes should not have loose threads.

- Do not use plastic belts that are meant to look like leather.

- Thread colour must match exactly (if that is the intention) and should be the same material as the garment.

- Prints and plaids must be matched at the seams.

- Fabrics should be natural or blends that look like natural fabrics.

Grooming Tips

- Shower daily and change your brand of deodorant regularly. Watch the powdered kind which can leave visible marks on clothes.

- Use a good skincare routine.

- Deal with excess facial, nostril and neck hair, rogue eyebrow hairs, and warts. (M)

- Always wear make-up for business, even on dress-down days. (W)

- Watch for lipstick on teeth. (W)

- Take care of hands and nails.

- Visit your hairdresser regularly (every six weeks) and remember – Cut, Colour, Condition.

- Exercise regularly, even if it is just running up the stairs instead of using the lift.

- Drink plenty of water and try to cut down on quick fixes of caffeine and nicotine.

- Visit your dentist and hygienist regularly.

- Well-fitted lingerie/underwear ensures that your clothes hang to their best advantage.

- Accessorize with well-chosen, good-quality pieces.

Emergency Grooming Kit

- Hair care products.

- Hair and clothes brushes.

- Spare tights. (W)

- Spare tie. (M)

- Make-up repair kit. (W)

- Toothpaste, toothbrush and dental floss.

- Body spray.

- Deodorant.

- Concealer.

- Breath spray.

- Nail file.

- Eye drops for red or tired eyes.

- Sewing kit – ready threaded with both black and white thread.

If you feel you need more help or some expert guidance on a one-to-one basis then I have two recommendations. Use the personal shoppers provided in many of the big department stores now when you go shopping for clothes. You will need to make a prior appointment, usually a few weeks ahead. Personal shoppers are a great help in opening up your mind to different designs and styles to suit you, and they also know their product range well. You need to give them an idea of what type of clothes you are looking for, and a budget to work to. The service is complimentary and you should not feel obligated to buy at the end.

Visiting an Image Consultant

For a more in-depth personal consultation you should invest in some time with an Image Consultant. Many people I have had the pleasure of advising over the years on a one-to-one basis have taken the time to tell me what a life-changing experience their session was, how their confidence and self-esteem improved and how it has made shopping easier. Many say that they wish that they had done it years ago! Hence, I do recommend taking a three-hour session with a qualified Image Consultant, but do make sure the consultant is suitably experienced and can advise you in areas related to business dress and impact too. Some consultants are not experienced in business image, so you should be careful to check this and ask what their background and experience is.

Important Questions to Ask and What to Expect

- When enquiring, ask for a consultant experienced in professional men's or women's image. Tell them you need to improve your business image and would like to spend time on this.

- How much will it cost? You can expect to pay upwards from £160 per session, depending on geographic location.

- What do you need to take with you? It is always useful to take a couple of outfits or suits with you (not half the contents of your wardrobe, though!) – one you feel really good in and another that you never feel comfortable in. A selection of ties for the men is good too.

- Women, ask if you will be having your make-up done. Take along your make-up bag and revamp it while there. Most consultants will stock products.

- Most consultants will have their own studio or some will come to your house. This can be useful if you'd like to have your wardrobe weeded out at the same time. Ask for hourly rates for this.

- Most consultants offer a personal shopping service – ask about hourly rates for this too.

- It can be useful to take a friend or partner with you to the consultation. They can also absorb all the advice to aid you with shopping later, although it should all be written down clearly for you. You should never be expected to strip off down to your underwear – body shape can easily be checked out while you are fully clothed.

- In a full session, you should expect:
  - A critique of first impressions.
  - Business image advice.
  - A full colour analysis with colour swatches.
  - Recommendations of styles for your body shape for business and social occasion – written notes.
  - Hair and grooming advice.
  - Accessory advice.
  - Advice on current trends.

chapter 4

Casual Power

NO MATTER WHAT YOUR IQ LEVEL OR JOB title, interpreting those dreaded words 'dress down', 'business casual' or 'smart casual' gives you an added challenge to your working week. It means that you no longer have a 'uniform' to rely on. Even with its recent entry to the *Oxford English Dictionary* 'dress down' still remains confusing to even the most sartorially competent of businessmen and women. Business is becoming much more global and we find ourselves working alongside Americans, Europeans and colleagues from the Middle and Far East, face to face and through web and video conferencing, on a regular basis. This makes it all the more important to have a flexible business wardrobe that will take you anywhere in the world and still command respect. Americans have been used to a dress-down culture for longer than us

Europeans, and the continental Europeans have traditionally been more comfortable with the concept, and have been stylish in their approach. Whatever your culture and whoever you deal with in business, you can make more mistakes with dress down than in suited attire. You need to emanate as much power, authority and credibility and command as much respect as you do in a suit, and this should not be difficult if you consider that confidence also comes from within, and not with a suit, attached like spare buttons! Going without the suit does not have to mean going without the attributes of personal power. However, for some reason, business casual gives us many problems. You can, of course, choose to ignore my advice in this chapter, believing that business casual is easy and constitutes what you wear at the weekends. This would suggest that you are not concerned with your career progression and chances for greater exposure in your job – but, given that you have bought this book, you obviously are concerned with these matters. Although the dress code phenomenon spreads across businesses in all sectors, it still causes one of the most confusing and ambiguous issues for business men and women. If I ask delegates in my presentations or respondents in research for a description of business casual, I get answers along the lines of:

- Weekend clothes
- Suit without a tie
- No jacket
- What you want to wear
- Jeans and sweatshirts.

I rarely see a description that includes any reference to commanding respect and retaining credibility, which, if you think about it, really are the elements at the root of the reason why the concept of business casual causes such a problem for UK business professionals. I believe the best way to sum up business casual is:

Dressing casually while being appropriate, exuding credibility, personal power and authority, and commanding respect – the look of quality.

GQ Editor Dylan Jones said (for Austin Reed): 'Dressing down with style causes you to take more care with your clothes; it means you don't have to wear a uniform every day, but stops you looking like the office scarecrow'.

One of the reasons that this has been such a problem is that businesses have followed in the new trend and have announced dress-down codes or casual Fridays, with little, if any, advice or training to staff on standards and expectations. This in turn has caused businesses to lose some of their identity and has put their corporate image in jeopardy. If we see a company filled with untidy-looking individuals we tend to associate sloppy business practices with them too. As we know, 'dress' is a powerful business tool and staff reflect the corporate image to the outside world to a large extent through this medium. Even some Fortune 100 companies struggle to balance professionalism and credibility with a business casual dress code. When a company has decided to adopt a dress-down code, the focus has tended to be on employee morale and productivity rather than on the external image of the company. An absence of guidance lays the land wide open to misinterpretation and poor judgement, and encourages professionally unacceptable gear to make its way through the office door – and it does. So, it is essential for company bosses to ensure that their corporate dress code continues to reflect the desired image. For us as individuals, we have to make sure that we still exude power, credibility and style, and business casual is another way to radiate your personality too. This chapter is aimed at helping to end the casual power confusion, and at assisting you to pump up personal power with your business casual wardrobe. Many of the tips in Chapter 3, particularly in respect of grooming, should still be applied to your business casual dress, and this chapter builds on the content there.

Let us simplify things – to start with, I am going to stick my neck out and announce that, in business terms, business casual is the same as smart casual. I believe that by having two terms (some books even give up to six terms for different levels of casual dress) we just confuse the issue even more. We just need to understand what look is 'appropriate'. Only you can decide that, given your business day ahead. 'Smart' always goes without saying, but we need to establish what is appropriate for *business* and what is going to propel you forwards in your career and not hold you back. 'Casual' is easy but it's getting the business balance right that can be tricky. So, from here on, I am going to refer only to 'business casual'.

In this chapter I'm going to give you some rules – as much about elements that constitute business casual as the definite no-nos. The rules here are not designed to intimidate or patronize but rather to make sure that you don't leave the house looking like you've dressed in the dark! These rules are designed as a base to work with, for you to then add a healthy measure of your own personality, a splash of your corporate image and a good helping of appropriateness for the situation, resulting in a truly powerful and professional total image for today's cutting-edge business world. My aim is that by providing you with these rules to adhere to, building a business casual wardrobe becomes much easier and the finished collection is more versatile. This new workwear revolution is not rocket science – all you need to do is to treat casual clothes with the respect you pay to formal clothes. Dressing down properly means that you could actually become a better dresser because of it.

Let's start by testing your casual power:

Are You Making the Desired Impact on Dress-down Days?

- Do you ever apologize, or have you wanted to apologize, for the way you're dressed when meeting with a client?

- Have your choices of dress-down gear ever stopped you from meeting with a client?

- Do you ever not shave/not wear make-up on dress-down days?

- Do you think of jeans and T-shirt or chinos and polo shirt as your staple dress-down wear (men)?

- Do you use dress-down as an excuse for wearing your summer dresses, low-cut tops, exposing pierced belly buttons and so on (women)?

- Have you ever under-dressed for business casual?

- Are you always thrown into turmoil when a business event states 'business casual' or 'smart casual' dress code?

- Do you wear your weekend sports casual or slobbing gear to the office?

- Have you ever adopted an 'it's good enough for work' attitude to your dress-down clothes?

- Have your clothes ever prompted a colleague (or worse, boss) to ask if you're only working a half-day?

If you have answered 'yes' to most of these or even any of these, then you could be jeopardizing your personal power on dress-down days – but don't worry, you are one of millions. This exercise has led you to consider and assess your business casual image and provides a good base to work from.

Your Company's Guidelines

As a corporate image consultant I have been called into companies of all sizes and in all sectors to offer advice and coaching on appropriate business casual dress and have seen all sorts of ambiguous memos from human resources (HR) departments attempting to describe a dress-down policy. Bizarrely enough, I have also seen message boards in offices apologizing for their dress code! One particular one, from a blue-chip company, read along the lines of:

> Dear Visitor, during your visit to our offices today you may encounter members of staff dressed in casual attire. This is quite normal and acceptable as we have introduced a policy permitting casual dress on Fridays. We trust that you will understand and that no offence will be caused.

It's a shame that this company could not put the effort into ensuring that their staff presented an appropriate image instead of making an embarrassing and laughable apology for it. As an HR director or owner of a company, it is difficult to clarify in words such an inherently paradoxical and emotive paradigm, not least due to the legal restrictions in place nowadays when managing personnel. It is even tougher to enforce and sustain a standard if clear guidelines have not been set.

Some companies will announce a dress-down code or casual Friday and give no useful standards to follow. This approach lays the whole concept wide open to misinterpretation and variations of perceived acceptability. Of course there are also those occasions when an event or training course states business casual or smart casual dress. From time to time, I provide image workshops for a Chamber of Commerce, and I clearly remember one session with eight male delegates. Unbeknown to me, the course confirmation stated 'Dress Code – Smart/Casual'. To reinforce my point on variations of perceived acceptability, we had one man in a suit and tie, two in jackets with open-necked shirts, three in plain shirts with no jacket, one in a brushed cotton shirt and one in a fleece! Apparently all these man thought they were dressed smart/casual. You cannot afford misinterpretation in business – it will cost you dearly in the personal power stakes. A similar thing happened when I was a guest speaker at a large conference for company directors last year – for the first time ever this particular conference was business casual during the day. Being on a cruise ship, we had a mixture of suits, casual shirts, T-shirts and even the odd pair of Bermuda shorts! One would think that top senior directors would have it sussed, but no, as I said earlier, IQ level and job title do not come into the equation.

Where there are no specific guidelines provided by a company you have a great opportunity to outshine your colleagues in the way you present yourself in business casual style. Hopefully this book will set you well down the road to achieving your desired impact.

Where your company has provided some guidelines to dress down, then I advise you to adhere to these if you have any regard for your future career and success. Remember this is not your mother telling you; you are employed to do your job and reflect the corporate image and you are expected to follow the dress standards that portray that image too. In fact, I wonder how many employment contracts now state 'must reflect the corporate image at all times' – it might be a good idea. Some dress policies state 'jeans, T-shirts and trainers are not acceptable'. Does this mean, then, that it is acceptable to turn up to the office in scruffy chinos that have lost their shape and a sloppy old shirt, or six earrings in one ear? I think not – that is, not if you value your career prospects. Your choices of clothes for dress down directly reflect your level of professionalism, your career plans and your respect for your workplace and employer.

Casual Friday

Or Funky Friday, as I have known it to be called in the US! For the bosses out there, I would like to pose one question for you . . . Why do you have Casual Friday? If it is to increase staff motivation or productivity then why not do it all week? And if you keep it to only one day because you believe standards become sloppy, why do it at all? Do not be led by industry trends, do what is right for your organization and corporate message. However, I do advocate an 'appropriate dressing' policy – considering what lies ahead for your business day. If you are meeting clients, then a jacket or suit is a must, and for days in the office then more casual attire is OK. But you should always be aware that unplanned meetings can occur, and therefore suitable clothes should always be kept in the office, just in case.

Casual Calamities

In many ways, understanding what to avoid for business casual is more helpful than being told what is right for you to wear. Avoid the definite no-nos, dress appropriately and bring out your personality make for a pretty safe bet. There are many ways in which you can destroy your casual power. Let me share with you some the classic mistakes that are made:

- Denim jeans (never professional, even with a jacket)
- Denim generally
- T-shirts in winter
- Cheap, logo-ed or sloganed T-shirts
- Motif print T-shirts under white shirts

- Trainers
- Sports clothes (jogging pants, sloppy T-shirts, tracksuits)
- Lack of grooming
  - Unclean/unstyled hair
  - Not shaving
  - No make-up
- Too much colour – can look clown-like
- Mixture of looks – for example, brogues with your chinos
- Jewellery overload
- White socks
- Leggings (women)
- Cowboy boots
- Anything unironed
- Clothes that you have labelled 'it'll do for work'
- Shorts (unless in an appropriate casual environment in a hot climate)
- High fashion and flesh-revealing garments (women)
- Bare legs
- Visible tattoos
- Shirts outside of trousers (men) (unless in the most casual of environments)
- Badly co-ordinated outfits
- Belief that a designer label is all that is needed to be smart
- Sandals of any form
- Body piercing
- Visible midriffs
- Sleeveless tops for men

- Strappy tops for women
- Visible underwear

All of these will diminish your credibility in the workplace and will highlight inconsistencies with your normal professional image when suited. This can cause people to believe that they have misjudged you and believe that you're not what they thought you were. Remember that dress-down day does not mean a licensed slob day!

Business Casual – what does it mean for me?

The level of business casual you go to depends on a number of elements, such as who you are meeting, the environment, the situation and what your objectives are for your day/meeting(s). My advice is to beware generally of business casual if meeting clients, particularly on their premises. It works best internally unless you know that your client's code is dress down too. Bear in mind the age of your clients – some older people sometimes don't feel respected if you're not wearing a suit. You have to judge whether you are going to portray the power and authority you need without your suit. When you have judged how formal or how casual a business situation is, then you can decide which types of clothes are appropriate. This next section describes for you a range of garments that are excellent business casual choices, and, by using the body shape and colour guidelines in Chapter 3, you can decide what is right for you, your job type and level and your day ahead.

Co-ordinating Separates

When you compare the ease of putting a suit and appropriate shirt/tie or top on in the morning to working out which jacket goes with which top/trousers/shoes and so on, then there is no doubt that a powerful suited look is far easier to create quickly than a powerful business casual one. The problem is that separates do not come with self-assembly instructions! So the perception is that we have to be creative, stylish *and* rich in order to have a totally co-ordinated business casual wardrobe that takes us through our working week with ease. Let us first dispel the myth that you have to have a high budget in order to be stylish. Just look at the number of celebs out there who leave a lot to be desired in the style department! With a few good-quality basic separates such as jackets and trousers, you can mix and match your wardrobe with moderately priced but well-chosen tops, shirts and accessories to provide you with a stylish yet versatile wardrobe. You do not have to buy designer everything (in fact, that is never a sure bet either) in order to ooze casual power.

Business Casual Essentials

Men

First and foremost, one of the biggest mistakes you can make is to mix your looks. What I mean by this is not wearing your formal suit with a casual, open-necked shirt, or your formal suit belt with your moleskins. You'll look slightly odd and certainly not well dressed. If you are dressing business casual, you must be consistent in your look, even down to the detail of belts and shoes.

Jackets

A jacket will always empower your look, but I don't mean taking your blazer and teaming it with your jeans. A suit jacket will always look like a suit jacket so you need at least three good-quality sports jackets in varying patterns and fabrics. You also need to choose jackets of appropriate fabric weights for summer and winter. If your idea of a business casual jacket is a navy blazer with brassy buttons, then think again. As mentioned previously, this will label you as dated and lacking in flair. Dark colours in jackets will always be more versatile, although it is good to have at least one lighter colour in the wardrobe. Unless you have a high budget and can afford to have several in your wardrobe, then avoid those colours and patterns that will limit your co-ordinating options. Business casual jackets will tend to be softer fabrics; there is a wide range available – the wool/linen/silk mixes are great, as is the new Tencel® often mixed with other natural fibres. Do be careful with pure silk or linen as these can crease badly, which rarely looks sharp in a business environment. However, you can often get away with wearing linen in a very casual environment or on the continent. Your business casual jackets should always be single-breasted – double-breasted has no place in casual style; it looks too formal. Look for jackets that have slit or patch pockets (pockets stitched on the outside) instead of trad-itional flaps. These will look more in keeping with the business casual look you want to portray. Wear your jackets with the bottom button undone and do treat your sports jackets the same way you would your best suits.

Because some men are reluctant to lose the formal suit, they will take the easy option and wear their normal suit, even if it is double-breasted, the same shirt, the same shoes but no tie. This just looks untidy. If you want to wear a suit, then you should choose one of the slightly less formal styles available, which are usually sold as separates. Again, linen, wool and silk mixes are popular in lighter and more relaxed colours and textures. One final point: always keep a jacket in the office in case of unplanned meetings with clients or the boss.

Shirts

Shirts worn outside of trousers are for weekends, not for retaining casual power in business, and if you're past 40 then you should con-sider avoiding this look at all costs. Your shirts should be of the same fine quality as those worn with your suits. Because they may be on view even more if you aren't wearing a jacket, then make sure they are well pressed. There are lots of wrinkle-free options available which will resist creasing for longer, and the better quality the cotton, the less creasing you will get. Oxford cloth, broadcloth and end-on-end are the ones to look out for. Pay particular attention to your collars – curling tips are not acceptable, even for your most casual days. Button-down collars are great for business casual, as they were never intended to be worn with a tie. Do make sure that the inside of your collars around the neck have not become discoloured – this will be visible if the neck is worn open. Plain colours are OK, but make sure you avoid wearing the formal white shirts that you would usually wear with a suit. You can go darker in shade and try some of the colours that are best for you. Also try some of the many patterns around in shirts now – stripes, checks and the styles with white collar and cuffs, which are still best kept for business casual and casual wear rather than formal wear. For a stylish and striking look, wear cufflinks with double-cuffed open-necked shirts – but make sure you wear a modern checked or striped shirt rather than shirts meant to be worn with a tie.

Trousers

Moleskin, corduroy, chinos, gabardine, wool worsted and cotton drill are good choices for business casual trousers. If your company dress policy states 'no jeans' then you would be best advised to avoid denim generally, even the smarter black types. Often moleskins or cords are in jean style – these are acceptable if they are kept in good condition. Flat-fronted trousers are popular, as are single-pleat styles, and if you choose tailored trousers with vertical creases then ensure that the creases are maintained. Drawstring, cargo and tech pants are suitable only for your most casual days in the office, and are not appropriate for client-facing environments.

Shoes

You should pick your business casual shoes carefully – they will have as much impact as your formal ones. You have choices of suede, slip-ons, loafer and moccasin slip-on styles, half-boots like Chelsea (pull-on styles) or slightly more formal Derby lace-ups. Cowboy boots are a no-no. Ensure that the style of your shoes complements the whole outfit and that your shoe wardrobe consists of brown or oxblood and black for business casual.

Knitwear

This is an option often missed, but worn without a jacket knitwear is a great choice for days in the office for a more relaxed look when you are not meeting clients. Merino wool and cashmere command the most casual power, and also look good under a jacket. Pure new wool and cotton yarns are acceptable too. Whatever you choose, make sure it is not sloppy or shapeless or you will be in danger of portraying a sloppy attitude too. Patterned and highly textured knits are suitable only for client-free days in the office. To keep your knitwear in good condition you should wash it by hand in a detergent suitable for wools, and lay it out flat to dry. It is excessive to wash knitwear after every wearing, so you need to keep a careful check on any unpleasant odours if you are wearing a garment two or three times. There are dry-cleaning products available now that you can use in the tumble dryer – they are great for freshening up garments. If you do sweat a lot then wear a vest or T-shirt underneath.

Business Casual is . . .

- Clean and pressed clothes
- Immaculate grooming – hair (clean and, if long, tied back), clean teeth and fresh breath, beards well groomed and nails clean and tidy

- Clothes in good condition, not 'past it' in terms of dated or scruffy

- Fine knits and jerseys

- Chinos, moleskins, cords, linen, cotton, gabardine and wool trousers

- Leather for jackets (blouson or reefer style), not trousers

- High-quality, logo-free T-shirts in summer

- Sports jackets in softer fabrics than your formal suits

- Crisp cotton and good-quality shirts

- Loafer-style shoes, half-boots, slip-ons

- Belts – leather or woven leather in casual style

Women

Men often say to me that 'it's easier for women, they have more choice'. But we could retaliate and say that 'it's easier for men, they have less choice'. It is fair to say that women have been putting separates together for business for longer, but we still have the same challenges as men, and perhaps even more so as credibility can be lost much more easily through our dress choices. Softly tailored separates are in abundance now in the shops, so think broadly and add a few to your business casual wardrobe. Take heed of the casual calamities earlier and use the following advice to avoid diminishing your casual power.

The Trouser Suit

This is widely accepted for both formal business and business casual, in all but perhaps the most traditional industries. It provides you with an extremely versatile base to your wardrobe and in neutral colours will be a wonderful investment. Edge-to-edge, collarless, zipped, military style and single button are great business casual options and work well when co-ordinated with fine wool or T-shirt-style tops. Boots can be worn with trousers but ones that are too funky or too high should be avoided.

Skirts

Business casual does not mean that your skirts or the slits in them can get higher – that is, if you do not want to lose respect and credibility fast. Always sit down in your skirts *before* you buy, to see just how far up they ride. Never wear short skirts with bare legs – you still need to wear fine-denier tights to be professional. Always make sure your skirts and trousers fit well, with about 4 cm either side at the seams – any tighter and they look cheap and unflattering. Sarongs should be kept for the beach.

Pseudo Jackets

Although there are many softer fabrics and deconstructed designs in jackets to choose from, there are alternatives for business casual. Short, knitted cardigans and tailored shirts (almost jacket style without the padded shoulders) can provide a versatile alternative for covering arms and for feeling that little bit more in control when necessary. And, yes, twin sets are still around, and if they are modern, fine quality and well accessorized, they look chic and sophisticated. Edge-to-edge designs are particularly popular and are a less fussy option.

Tops

From T-shirt-style tops to shirts and ladies' cufflinks – the choice is vast. You have a great opportunity to wear some of your best accent colours in patterns and textures for added interest and impact. Sleeveless and strappy tops are OK under jackets, but invariably you will take your jacket off and expose credibility-losing flesh. Your underwear should never be visible underneath your tops nor should you wear tops without underwear.

Business Casual is . . .

- Clean and pressed clothes

- Immaculate grooming – clean hair and tied back if long, clean teeth and fresh breath, unchipped nails, make-up

- Clothes in good condition, not 'past it' in terms of dated or scruffy

- Softly tailored suits and jackets

- Trouser suits

- Fine knits and jerseys

- Accent-colour tops and shirts

- Leather for jackets and coats, not trousers or skirts

- High-quality, logo-free T-shirts in summer

- Well-chosen and quality accessories

Some Common Mistakes that Women Make

- Florals
- Heavily patterned skirts or trousers
- Chunky and frumpy shoes
- Over-the-top jewellery
- Low-cut and/or strappy tops
- Flimsy fabrics

Examples and Scales of Business Casual

Sometimes it is difficult to ascertain the level of business casual to go to. These scales for men and women may help.

For Men

Starting with the most formal combinations and ending with the most casual:

- Suit in softer fabric with casual, open-necked shirt
- Suit as above with T-shirt or knitwear

- Sports jacket and tailored trousers with casual, open-necked shirt
- Sports jacket and tailored trousers with T-shirt, polo shirt or knitwear
- Tailored trousers with checked or striped casual, open-necked shirt
- Tailored trousers with T-shirt, polo shirt or knitwear
- Moleskins, chinos or cords with casual, open-necked shirt
- Moleskins, chinos or cords with T-shirt, polo shirt or knitwear

A blouson or reefer-style jacket in suede, leather or moleskin can be added where no other jacket is mentioned. Anything off the end of the scale is going to be either too formal and therefore not appropriate for business casual or far too relaxed and sloppy.

For Women

Starting with the most formal combinations and ending with the most casual:

- Softly tailored trouser suit with shirt and cufflinks
- Softly tailored trouser suit with accent-colour top
- Co-ordinated separates of skirt/trousers and jacket with accent-colour top
- Dress with softly tailored jacket
- Dress with fine-knit cardigan
- Trousers/skirt with knitwear (cardigan or twin set)
- Trousers/skirt with T-shirt-style top

To retain casual power, all the above need careful accessorizing. Classic-style court shoes can be worn with all to formalize the look more. Boots or loafer styles can be worn with trousers, and knee-length boots with skirts if appropriate to the look. Avoid wearing flat shoes with skirts – this never looks professional.

Wardrobe Re-engineering

Hopefully, by this stage in the book, you have some clear ideas for your business casual wardrobe, as well as an understanding of your body shape, colouring and business wardrobe requirements. Before you rush out and invest in new gear, let me suggest that you do a little wardrobe feng shui or re-engineering first. You need to clear out the junk that is just cluttering up your view of what you have and limiting your scope for creating a versatile wardrobe. So, get yourself a glass of wine or bottle of beer, arm yourself with a few large bin liners and sticky white labels and make your way to your wardrobe. Let's take it in three steps:

Audit

Take out everything and see exactly what you have. Hang or lay it in groups of similar garments – that is, trousers, jackets, shirts, tops, shoes, accessories and knitwear. Anything that needs a repair, an alteration or a clean should be put to one side straight away, or binned if beyond help.

De-Junk

Now comes the hard bit. Label your bin liners: 'bin', 'charity shop', 'recycling' (clothes banks are now widely available), 'storage' and 'exchange shop'. Many towns now have exchange shops – they take in good-quality clothes in good condition and that are still saleable in terms of fashion, and sell them for you, taking a percentage of the sale. Now be ruthless.

- *Past its best?* – it has to go. It will serve only to diminish your image impact.
- *Dated?* – it also has to go. You are in real danger of portraying dated thought processes.
- *No longer fits?* – be realistic, and put into storage if necessary.

Only keep for storage those items that you cannot bear to throw away or think may come back into fashion, but don't be too optimistic!

Reorganize

So, what's left? Probably the 20 per cent of the wardrobe that you wear a lot, and a bit more, because you have now discovered garments that you had forgotten about or have now decided are good for your colouring, shape or will actually co-ordinate well with that new jacket. Women should hang skirts, trousers and jackets separately, to create more versatility. Put all your knitwear together, preferably in one of those wonderful canvas hanging shelves, so that you can see everything you have. Use cedar wood balls to protect your knits – they don't smell anywhere near as bad as mothballs. Put your business casual shirts and tops together and your formal shirts and tops in another section. For women, it will help you to co-ordinate your outfits if you put items in colour order too.

As you're going through this process you will start to see the gaps and items needing to be purchased to get the most out of your outfits. And finally, the best bit (for some anyway!).

Reinvest

Having restructured your wardrobe and established the gaps, you can now reinvest wisely. No longer will you be so tempted by so-called half-price bargains; you'll go shopping knowing what you're looking for, and that is great if it's also in the sale.

If you need new suits, be prepared to buy new shirts, ties and tops as well if possible. It really helps with co-ordinating.

Good luck and enjoy!

The form on p. 133 may help with your wardrobe re-engineering. Use it to record what you have, what goes with what and to highlight what you need.

GARMENT	GOES WITH (already have)	NEED TO PURCHASE
Jackets		
Trousers		
Shirts		
Tops		
Knitwear		

Continued

GARMENT	GOES WITH (already have)	NEED TO PURCHASE
Shoes		
Belts		
Over-jackets		
Dresses		

chapter 5

Body 'Talk'

B ODY LANGUAGE IS A USEFUL TOOL WHEN you learn that not only can it help you get on in business by reinforcing positive words with confidence and assertiveness, but it can also enable you to look *beyond* the words that others use and get to the real agenda inside. Most researchers in this subject agree that we mainly use the verbal content of our message to convey information and the non-verbal element is used to understand personal attitudes. As our body language is controlled largely by the subconscious, the assumption is that it gives honest clues and indicators into somebody's inner self, even though the words may be giving conflicting messages. Imagine wearing a blindfold in a meeting: how do you know when somebody wants to speak, is bored, enthusiastic or uninterested? If you use conference call facilities and video conferencing, where the whole body often is not visible, you will know only too well how difficult it is to interpret people's attitudes and reactions to what you are saying. As we already know, Mehrabian (1971) found that about 55 per cent of the impact we make is focused on our visual 'package', so it makes sense to use it to its greatest advantage, to be aware of it and to modify our gestures to be conducive to effective communication. Body language, then, is a powerful aid to making positive impact, but is also a potential hazard to get in the way of your desired message. It really is the unspoken truth.

This chapter will give you some specifics about body language as a tool for effective and positive communication. I am going to focus on the aspects that are *key* to your image impact and on areas that will help you to:

- Be more assertive
- Build credibility, trust and respect
- Improve your interpersonal skills
- Be more aware of negative gestures in yourself and others
- Carry greater influence
- Be more confident
- Highlight hidden agendas and silent messages in others
- Enhance effective communication.

Intuition

We talk about people as being intuitive or perceptive, or we describe our 'gut' reactions – but what does this mean? Everybody hears the same words, but some people are just able to pick up specific or additional messages from the non-verbal clues they have received. We often have a hunch that somebody is not telling us the complete truth because their spoken words and their body language are inconsistent. Research shows that non-verbal signals carry about six times more impact than the verbal messages and that when the two are inconsistent we trust the non-verbal signals and the verbal message is often disregarded. We are more likely to believe what we *see* than what we *hear* – we feel uncomfortable and a level of distrust is created if the words are inconsistent with the silent messages. Women are generally more perceptive than men, and we are all familiar with the term 'woman's intuition'. Women have a useful innate ability to decipher non-verbal signals and pick up on small details, whereas a man will observe the whole picture and will be less likely to notice small meaningful signs.

A 'Language'

I do believe that the subject of interpreting body language can get out of hand, so let's put things in perspective. There is a danger of unfairly judging somebody by failing to take an action or gesture in context, in just the same way as taking words out of the context of a sentence or situation they are meant to be surrounded by. Body language is just that, a language, not a series of words to be translated individually. For example, if somebody in your audience is crossing their arms across their body, then you could assume that they are defensive to your message and disagreeing with you. However, they may be cold and/or have a stomach pain. If, however, they consistently frown or sigh, then you are probably safe to assume that they are in disagreement. If this same person had legs and arms crossed in this way in a doctor's waiting room, you would assume that they are cold and not feeling too good. So make sure that it is fair to form your assumptions, and bear in mind the situation and context.

Cultural differences and variables are important to be aware of. It is arrogant to assume that all countries of the world will understand your body language and gestures. I have included some cultural differences at the end of this chapter and I would strongly advise that you read up on other cultures before travelling to specific countries and parts of the world to do business, and before hosting foreign guests, to familiarize yourself with the major differences.

So, what is going to stand in the way of positive body talk? Let's start by asking you a few questions to see how well you already interpret body language signals. I must stress here, however, that none of these gestures should be taken in isolation but rather in context and with other gestures. This exercise is designed to give you some indicators of the usual meaning of common body language signals. Put yourself in each situation and work out how you would interpret the signals:

1. You're sitting opposite a client in an office and he/she is sitting back in the chair with their arms crossed.

2. The client then leans forward towards you, uncrosses their arms and leans on the desk.

3. During the conversation the client leans away from you but leaves his hands on the desk.

4. When you're talking to someone they put their hands out with palms up.

5. While you're speaking, your client leans forward, puts his elbows on the table and puts his fingertips together to form a steeple effect.

6. While you're speaking, your client sits back in his chair with his hands clasped behind his head.

7. Your client intermittently moves his hand around over his mouth while he's speaking.

8. As *you're* speaking your client puts his hand over his mouth.

9. As he's speaking, your client rubs his ear.

10. As you're speaking, your client, while sitting down, puts his hands on his thighs/knees as if he's about to stand up.

11. While you're talking in a meeting, somebody puts their elbow on the table and leans their fist against their cheek.

12. The other person is constantly fiddling with a pen while he/she is speaking.

So how did you do?

1. Generally, arms crossed means defensive or negative response. This person could be in disagreement with what you're saying, or needs to be convinced.

2. Leaning forward suggests interest and agreement with what you're saying. They are also comfortable with you. For further clarification of this, watch to see whether the pupils dilate too.

3. Leaning away from you could mean disagreement with what you're saying again, although to be certain you need to watch other gestures. It could just be that he is changing positions.

4. Palms up usually means somebody is being honest and open. However, if exaggerated or out of context, it can mean dishonesty. For example, imagine somebody saying to you with palms up and a shrug of the shoulders, 'come on, believe me . . .'!

5. Placing the fingertips together to form a raised steeple is a sign of superiority and confidence. You can use this gesture to regain control in a meeting. Often people who use minimal body gestures will use this one frequently.

6. The hands behind the head is a very strong superiority gesture. A sort of 'I'm in control here' or 'you can't fool me' signal. With one leg over

the other in a figure 4 position, it implies a very arrogant 'some day you'll be as good as me' message.

7. The hand moving over the mouth of the talker suggests that he's nervous about what he's saying, as if he's trying to hide the words or the truth. Notice that children do this but tend to cover their whole mouth, teenagers are slightly better at it by touching the mouth with their fingers and as adults we tend to maybe just scratch the chin or rub the lips occasionally.

8. The hand over the mouth of the listener can mean a few different things and these should be noted. It can mean that he wants to speak, or believes you're not telling the truth or is uncomfortable with what he is hearing.

9. Rubbing the ear, scratching the nose or chin or picking imaginary lint from clothes give similar messages. They suggest nervousness and discomfort with the situation, and possibly boredom.

10. Hands on knees or thighs suggest that the person wants to stand up and end the conversation.

11. When the head is supported by the hand in this way, this usually means the person is bored and uninterested. If you sense this, then getting up and using the flipchart adds a new level of interest to the discussion.

12. Constant fiddling with anything while talking suggests significant discomfort with what you're saying, and possible dishonesty.

These are just a few of the important body language gestures to look out for and then *act* on to retain credibility and control of a situation. If you're not sure how to interpret somebody's feelings or reactions to what you're saying, it is important to ask questions to clarify, such as 'how do you feel about that?' or 'how does that sound to you?' If somebody is looking particularly defensive, with arms crossed, then give them something to hold – for example, pass them a document and say, 'what do you think of this, John?'

Now, let's take the key body language gestures and elaborate on their meanings and how to use them to greatest effect.

Posture

Let's face it, bad posture is not only bad for you but it makes you look older and fatter too. If you want to be seen as somebody who is ready for business, confident and in control, then your posture needs to reflect this. Sloppy, slouchy posture will give people a clear message that you have less than high-quality standards in your approach to business. Good posture makes you feel more confident, improves self-esteem and leaves you looking slimmer, taller and more toned   I'm up for that! I only have to look at the way the people I've provided make-overs for on TV (some of whom have a very low self-image) walk out into the studio afterwards to know how good they now feel about themselves. If your shoulders are naturally rounded, always wear jackets with light padding to square up and sharpen up. When stand-ing, your jacket done up will give better posture and also serve to keep attention in the face area, or influencing triangle. Buttoning up keeps attention away from any distractions around the midriff area too, pro-viding that the jacket fits well and hangs evenly when done up. Learn to adopt a balanced position with feet well planted on the ground, when sitting too, with your shoulders relaxed and arms and legs uncrossed. This posture will allow your body to move freely and easily too. If you're looking tense, then you will appear insecure and nervous. Learn to adopt a position that looks relaxed and comfortable without looking sloppy.

The Alexander Technique is one of the most effective ways to improve posture. The key is learning how to balance your head freely on top of your spine. Pilates also helps as it strengthens the body and increases postural control.

Eye Contact

We learned at an early age that eye contact is polite and important when our mothers would say, 'look at me when I'm talking to you' – remember that? We know that we feel uncomfortable, irritated and invisible when somebody doesn't look at us when we're talking. They come across as uninterested, ill mannered, not listening and, some say, 'shifty' – all these negatives add up. 'The eyes are the windows to the soul' is the old adage and, in the words of Agatha Christie's Hercule Poirot, 'your eyes betray what your tongue denies'. When we interact with people one to one, we should be retaining eye contact for about 80 per cent of the time when listening and for about 40 per cent of the time when talking. Our eyes move around a lot more when we are talking because we think in terms of pictures, feelings and sounds. For example, if we are visualizing something from our past experience our eyes tend to move up and to the left, and if we are trying to access feelings and thoughts then our eyes move to the right and down. Studies show that our brains are split into two halves – the right brain and the left brain. The right brain handles pictures, colour, imagination, creativity, music, patterns, spatial awareness and intangibles. The left brain handles logic, language, mathematics, analysis, statistics, sequencing and numbers. These descriptions relate to most right-handed people and some left-handed people. To experience what I mean by this, think about walking into your bedroom and opening the wardrobe doors – what do you see first? Did you feel that your eyes moved up and to the left to *visualize* this picture? Now try to imagine yourself in full leathers, riding a Harley-Davidson along Pacific High-way in California. Did you notice that your eyes went up and to the right to *create* the picture? Unless, of course, you have a *memory* of this! When we access the kinaesthetic part of our brain, our eyes will move down and to the right – try thinking about holding a soft, fluffy toy. And when appealing to our auditory senses, our eyes move across to our right ear – for example, what happens to your eyes when I say 'what would your colleagues say about your ability to present to an audi-ence?' Again, these examples are true for most right-handed people, and most left-handed people do it in reverse. So, when the other per-son's eyes move away from us it does not always mean that they are uninterested, they are merely accessing areas of the brain to visualize pictures or form auditory or kinaesthetic emotions. This is another example of how body language should be kept in context.

The pupils also indicate to you how interested somebody is in what you are saying. When the pupil dilates, the person is indicating a degree of interest or excitement in what they are seeing, feeling or hearing. When the pupils contract, they are showing a lack of interest.

We should also be aware that unbroken eye contact can be intimi-dating and make your audience feel uncomfortable, so break yours occasionally. Here is a tip if you find it difficult to retain eye contact: try looking *between* the eyes rather than *directly at* the eyes. This will work well if you are 4 feet or more away from the other person, although it does feel odd. It is a useful option to bear in mind though.

As we obviously communicate more effectively by using good eye contact, it makes sense not to obscure them in any way. Choose non-reflective and non-tinted lenses for your office glasses and do not over-power or hide your eyes with heavy make-up or long, cascading fringes.

Handshake

In my experience very few people have ever received feedback on their handshake – which is bizarre when it is one of the first things you do when meeting somebody for the first time, and we know how important first impressions are. So, to start with, get feedback *now*. I find that when I do this exercise in my workshops, even though people are trying harder to get it right, there are still some that have handshakes that are bone-crushers or limp, wet fish! People often say to me, 'I never know *when* to shake hands'. For men *and* women in a business situation it always shows confidence and professionalism to initiate a handshake when being introduced or introducing yourself to somebody. If it is appropriate to shake hands, then go for it. For example, if you are a secretary or a PA greeting a client in your offices, it is polite and appropriate to shake hands and introduce yourself. However, if you're going into an interview with a panel of interviewers, then it may not be feasible to shake everybody's hands. You must use your judgement. A normal handshake should last for about 3–4 shakes: any more and you will appear over-friendly, and any less and you will appear dismissive. You should bear in mind that I am talking here primarily about the British, European and US cultures, and handshake styles will vary throughout the world. Greeting styles even differ regionally in the UK. For example, while it is quite normal to greet somebody you've met before with a kiss on the cheek in cosmopolitan London, if you do the same in the north of England you're likely to meet with a look of disapproval, although I'm sure this will change in due course. Your handshake does imply a lot about you as a person, so let's look at the ineffectual ones, which can lose you credibility in the first few seconds:

The Limp Loser

Strong title, but it is a fact that a limp handshake will label you as weak in character and 'a bit of a pushover'. Men should not weaken their handshake excessively for women.

The Wet Fish

This just leaves you wanting to dash to the bathroom and wash your hands – not pleasant. A sweaty palm is not the lasting impression you want to give. Combine a wet fish with a limp loser and you have just sabotaged your chances of making a positive impact. Use a dry-spary antiperspirant before an important meeting – it'll work the same as it does on the body.

The Bone-Crusher

This just comes across as arrogant and gives a 'tough guy' image, as well as possibly leaving a lasting and agonizing impression on the other person.

Double-handed

This is often called the politician's handshake, and is when the left hand covers the other person's right hand on handshake. It is supposed give a sincere and trustworthy impression, but exactly the opposite tends to come across. Most people do not feel comfortable with this, so be careful when you use it.

When to Kiss and When Not to Kiss

This is becoming more of an issue for some people as we increasingly mix with other cultures in business. My advice is to stick to the hand-shake in business unless the relationship has become a personal friend-ship, in which case kissing is OK. To decide this, consider whether you would invite this person to a party at your home – if the answer is 'yes', then your relationship is probably kissable. If you would invite this person to dinner, then your relationship is definitely kissable. Men to men, however, should still stick to shaking hands. Do be prepared for a kiss on both cheeks at least once from the continental Europeans and don't be completely taken aback – just watch the body language and try to respond in time.

Smiling

There is nothing unusual about a smile except the effect it has – it is perhaps one of the most powerful tools of expression you have. It gains you respect from others and gives you inner and outer confidence too. It breaks down barriers and awkward situations. A smile dominates your face and gives an indication to the other person of how you are feeling, and everybody likes to deal with happy, confident people. Of course, be careful not to overdo it, but reacting in an appropriate way to humour from others will win you friends and self-assurance. Studies have shown that about one-third of business people have naturally open and smiley faces. Another third have neutral faces and the remaining third have serious and intense faces. Find out from friends and colleagues which third you fall into. You probably think that you are smiling more than you actually are. If you fall into the lower third then it is time to do some work on this – whether you are smiling on the inside or not, you will be reflecting doom and gloom on the outside. Remember, perception is reality in the eye of the beholder. If you don't find it easy to smile then practise smiling in front of the mirror. What seems exaggerated to you probably is not exaggerated at all, but it has to be genuine and not cheesy. The best way to practise smiling is to raise the cheekbones rather than moving the lips. We know that smiling is infectious and is easily passed on to others – how powerful is that? Do judge for yourselves when it is appropriate, though – I don't want to be held responsible for unfortunate encounters with strangers in the street! One last point on smiling – do make sure that your teeth do not diminish the potential power of your smile. As mentioned earlier, check them and treat them regularly.

Irritating Gestures

You can easily draw attention away from what you are saying by engaging in distracting and irritating gestures. These you will no doubt do subconsciously, so ask colleagues to give you feedback on how you conduct yourself when speaking, both in meetings and in presentations. I know that I have been amazed at some of the distractions I have adopted in the past that I had not been aware of, which colleagues have told me about or which have been proved on video! Here are some of the most irritating gesture traps that people often fall into when meeting others:

- *Pen twiddling* – You will appear nervous and uncomfortable. Place your pen deliberately down on the table at the top of your paper or file to avoid the temptation to fiddle.

- *Doodling* – You are in danger of appearing distracted and uninterested in the proceedings. Again, place your pen deliberately down out of reach.

- *Picking off imaginary fluff from clothes* – This is an annoying habit for others and you will come across as very nervous and anxious.

- *Scratching chin, ear, nose* – If this is done repeatedly then you will create a feeling among others that you are hiding something or being dishonest. It indicates that you are not comfortable with what you are saying. When trust, respect and credibility are key to projecting a positive image, then you've blown it if this is you.

- *Collar/tie fiddling* – You will indicate that you are feeling a little 'hot under the collar' and uncomfortable with the situation.

- *Nervous cough* – It is probably just that, and you're probably completely unaware of it. If it starts just as you start to give your input, then you will definitely be considered to be lying.

- *Lip licking* – If this is done continuously then it suggests that you're feeling unsure about your words.

Mirroring

This is an effective tool for bonding and building rapport with another person. The secret is not to appear to mimic but rather to appear at ease with the other person by copying their movements a few seconds or a couple of minutes after, rather than immediately. If you watch two men standing at a bar drinking, you can guarantee that when one picks up his pint the other will do the same within a second or two. This shows that they are relaxed in one another's company. To give an example of a situation where two people are not relaxed with each other, imagine a meeting with a client: your client is sitting back in his chair with his fingertips together in a steeple effect and you are leaning forward with your elbows on the table – you are going to appear aggressive. If you were to match his posture and gestures, then the atmosphere would relax and be more conducive to effective communication. The more you match, the greater the opportunity to then lead. If you are communicating well and the level of rapport is sufficiently good, the other person will start to match your movements too.

Your language can also be matched to another person's for building rapport. I mentioned earlier about the various eye positions when imagining visions, feelings or sounds. People also use these language bases to communicate verbally:

- Visual – thinking in pictures
- Kinaesthetic – thinking in feelings
- Auditory – thinking in sounds

Some words and phrases that each type typically uses:

- *Visual*
  - I see what you're saying
  - That's very clear to me
  - That looks good to me
- *Kinaesthetic*
  - It doesn't feel right to me
  - I feel I need to . . .
  - I haven't quite grasped your idea yet
- *Auditory*
  - I hear what you're saying
  - I think my people will be able to tune into that
  - That sounds good to me

By being aware of another person's preferred language base you can match that and get your message across to them with much more impact. They will be able to relate more to what you're saying and to feel that they are on your wavelength. Listen out for obvious language base clues. This concept relates to a technique called Neuro Linguistic Programming (NLP). There are many books that enable you to read further into this fascinating and useful subject.

Aggressive v Assertive Gestures

I'm sure that many of you will have attended courses on 'Assertive-ness', as it is something we all strive for, but putting it into action is the difficult bit. Your body language has a lot to do with whether you come across as assertive or as aggressive. I will always remember a young and dynamic sales manager in a company I worked with who came across particularly aggressively because of one particular gesture he used fre-quently. When members of his sales team wanted to talk to him, he would tell them that he didn't have much time and then proceed to do a count-down signal with his thumb and index finger, gradually bringing the thumb and finger closer together. This came to light in my work-shop session when his team chose to confront him with it. They were understandably annoyed by it but the sales manager had no idea just how much arrogance and aggression he was displaying. Needless to say, this particular aggressive gesture was curbed and the relationship between him and his team improved.

Aggressive Gestures

- Finger pointing

- Standing too close to someone

- Frowning

- Hands behind head and feet on the desk

- Staring

- Bone-crushing handshake

- Over-erect posture and chest stuck out

- Making a fist

- Hands on hips

- Pacing when talking or being spoken to

- Crossed arms

- Chin up

- Narrowed eyes

- A false and exaggerated smile

- Over-talking and little listening

Assertive Gestures

- Genuine smile

- Firm handshake

- Good eye contact

- Open hand gestures

- Balanced and upright posture

- Appropriate gestures to back up verbal content

- Listening

In summary, here is my quick checklist for making positive impact with your body language. Tick these when you have received some feedback from others and have mastered these basics.

Posture

☐ Relaxed and balanced

☐ Avoid crossing arms and legs and looking generally tense

☐ Use the Alexander Technique to improve where necessary

☐ If you have rounded shoulders, avoid jackets that have sloppy shoulder lines

Eye Contact

☐ Your eyes are a great tool for getting your message across. Make sure they accentuate what you are saying

☐ Retain eye contact when people are speaking direct to you and learn to break it appropriately too

Gestures

☐ Use hand and arm movements to accentuate what you have to say

☐ Avoid irritating and negative signals like scratching the chin, picking off imaginary fluff etc.

☐ Avoid, at all costs, gestures that imply lying

☐ Use smiling effectively

A Few Cultural Differences

There are a few gestures that could get you into trouble in other countries, and I stress again the importance of checking up in detail on this before you visit or entertain guests from other cultures. However, you may find these few key points useful. They refer to what I consider to be the most commonly asked questions about meeting and greeting people and represent some of the biggest personal first impression blunders you can make in foreign business.

India

- Avoid pointing.
- Western women should avoid initiating handshakes with Indian men.

Israel

- Avoid crossing legs and showing soles of shoes.
- Avoid pointing.

Japan

- Sometimes bow to greet each other but are usually used to shaking hands with Westerners. If bowing, just use the head and place both hands on your thighs and lower your eyes: 2–3 times is normal.

- The handshake may not be a firm grip and the eyes may be averted.
- Eye contact is indirect.
- Women are taught never to look a man in the eye.
- Not tactile, so avoid kissing and touching the arm when shaking hands.
- When giving and receiving business cards, use both hands and study the one given to you before carefully putting away.
- Have a translation of your business card printed on the reverse.
- Do not blow your nose in public.
- Avoid pointing.
- Do not laugh loudly in meetings and avoid aggressive gestures.

Malaysia

- Eye contact is indirect.
- It is considered very rude to cross your legs, exposing the soles of your shoes.

The Netherlands

- Will often kiss three times when they have met you a few times.
- They are very forthright and expressive which can make them appear aggressive.

The Philippines

- Avoid crossing arms or putting hand on your chin.

Poland

- Men will sometimes kiss a woman's hand. Accept graciously and do not get irritated.

- Direct eye contact is absolutely essential.

Portugal

- Will kiss both cheeks, even if they have not met you before.

Russia

- Bear hugs among men are not uncommon. It is a sign of friendship.

Saudi Arabia

- Women should avoid initiating handshakes.
- Avoid pointing.
- Avoid crossing legs with soles showing – it is a great insult.

Singapore

- Eye contact is indirect.
- Avoid pointing.
- Avoid arms crossed in front of the body.

South Korea

- Koreans greet by bowing, but sometimes two men will shake hands.
- Eye contact is indirect.
- Avoid pointing and any flamboyant gestures.

Spain

- When they know you, the Spaniards will kiss on both cheeks.

Thailand

- Often greet each other by placing hands together, bowing slightly.
- Used to shaking hands with Westerners.
- Avoid crossing legs.
- Eye contact is indirect.

chapter 6

Are You Being Heard?

S O, YOU HAVE SEEN THE POWER OF NON-verbal communication in terms of appearance and body language, but what about your voice? There is little point in *looking* confident if your voice gets in the way of projecting quality. Because your voice quality represents about 38 per cent of the impact you make, you have to ensure that it is consistent with your personal brand values. Research shows that businesspeople get hung up with and worry about the words they use but pay little attention to the way their voice comes across, yet the words themselves have less impact than the voice and the rest of the personal package. In your opening lines, your audience will decide how trustworthy you are and whether you're worth listening to.

In Chapter 7: Added Impact Presentations, I

have included a self-analysis questionnaire, which includes voice quality. You should use this to check out how your voice comes across to others. You should also record your voice and hear for yourself. Recording on something digital rather than tape will give you a truer refection of the sound of your actual voice. The elements you need to look for are:

- Strength
- Control
- Resonance
- Intonation
- Clarity
- Articulation

- Volume
- Pace
- Modulation
- Emphasis
- Pitch

How well do you use all of these elements? If you have a severe problem with any of these areas, then I would advise visiting a voice coach – some contacts are listed at the back of the book. However, most moderate issues can easily be overcome.

Voice Preparation

If you are preparing for an important presentation, then you should also prepare the voice. You don't want to start your opening lines with a weak or croaky airing of words. It is important to relax the body and release tension beforehand, particularly in the face, neck and shoulders, as tension tightens the voice. Try some of these exercises – in private, of course!

- Circle your shoulders backwards a few times, then raise them up to your ears. Hold the tension there before you drop your shoulders down – then drop them down again. Ease your neck from side to side slowly –

looking over each shoulder; angle your head down to your shoulders each side, feeling a gentle stretch in your neck as you do so; and lastly drop your chin on to your chest, ease your head from side to side again, and then slowly bring your head up to its balanced, centred position.

- Open your mouth really wide and yawn. This stretches the mouth and muscles.

- Do a big, cheesy smile, raising your cheeks up high, and really stretch your mouth. Then pull your lips together as if about to say 'O' and push them out hard. Do these alternately five or six times. This gets the muscles around the mouth moving freely.

- Loosen your lips and blow through them, making a sound like a horse! Repeat three times.

- Give your jaw a gentle massage – imagine chewing gum and move your mouth around. Clean your teeth with your tongue and practise some tongue twisters.

Warm Up Your Voice

This is important before putting it under pressure, just as you would warm up any other muscles before using them strenuously for sport or exercise. If you don't do this, your voice could start off croaky and husky. Try humming – keep your lips, tongue and jaw loose. And 'sirening' – use the sound 'ng' as in 'sing' and gently slide your voice up and down its range, without straining.

Voice Impact

So now you're prepared, you need to be aware of the elements that can make a difference when speaking. All of these aspects apply to meetings, interviews, presentations and telephone conversations. You need to think about:

Clarity

Strength

Interest

We'll deal with each separately.

Clarity

Unless your voice is clear, there is little point in spending vast amounts of time preparing a speech, and, to be frank, little point in getting up and speaking. If people cannot hear what you're saying clearly, they will switch off in the first few minutes and their minds will stray to other things. Do not talk down to the floor or mumble, and keep a reasonable pace to your words. Articulate your words clearly – clarity of speech implies clarity of thought and it saves your voice.

Accents

If you have an accent, it can be a great asset to your personal brand. Think of it as an asset that distinguishes you from others and that makes you unique. However, do make sure that all your words are pronounced completely and don't miss off letters and sounds so that the speech appears sloppy and is hard to understand. Do not use any regional colloquialisms that are not easily understood in other parts of the country or abroad. If you do have a strong regional accent that you feel is getting in the way of your career progression, visiting a voice coach can help with this. I originated from Suffolk, England, and was the proud owner of this rather laid-back and relaxed accent – until, that is, I came to London to work. I then realized that if I wanted to be taken seriously, I had to work hard to lose some of the broadness of my accent. This I did over a period of time without the help of a coach. It now slips out only when back in Suffolk or when talking to my parents on the phone. Many well-known people have accents that they are proud of and in fact are famous for – for example, Janet Street-Porter,

Cilla Black and Jonathan Ross. Do remember, though, that if you have a pronounced accent, people whose native language is not English may have trouble understanding you.

Strength

If your voice is weak or quiet, people will assume that you are nervous, under-confident and ineffectual. A quiet voice is difficult to hear and understand and again your audience will quickly become bored with trying to hear.

Breathing more deeply will help you to have more strength in the voice. Follow the breathing exercise below before a presentation or before a challenging phone call, to help control the voice. Your breathing needs to come from your 'centre' – involving your diaphragm, stomach muscles and ribs. To get in touch with this:

- Sit back in your chair and relax your shoulders. Close your eyes, and rest one hand on your stomach. As you breathe in, feel your stomach moving outwards. As you breathe out, feel it moving inwards. Just focus on these movements for a few breaths.
- Slowly breathe in, counting to 2, and out, counting to 4. Do this several times, focusing on your outward breath, and feeling yourself letting go of tension with this.

Before you start speaking in a presentation, or before starting a challenging phone call:

- Breathe out – and let that tension go. Let your breath then naturally come in to support and calm you – and your voice.

Interest

Variety and interest are important if you are to hold your audience's attention and make an impact. Within the first 30 seconds an audience will decide how much attention they are going to give you. Make sure you pitch your voice at the right level – a harsh voice, shouting, high pitch or sarcasm in a voice will all switch an audience off. Try to establish rapport with your voice at the start.

Varying your pace, modulation and volume in a presentation are all necessary for engaging an audience's attention. Listen to a newsreader or TV presenter's voice and note the variation in the tone and the emphasis on certain words. These people are employed because of their ability to vary their voice appropriately and add interest to the storyline in a situation where there is often not the opportunity for extra emphasis with gestures and body language. The best way to assess how good you are at varying your voice is to use video feedback. Focus on how many times you manage to pause or change speed, volume or tone – could you add more, are you consistently too fast, are there too many pauses, and so on? Also try leaving yourself a couple of voicemail messages a week and focusing on one aspect of your voice at a time. You can also repeat well-known nursery rhymes or poems using a variety of tone and pitch, trying to add interest in different ways.

Highs and Lows

Nerves can often cause a speaker's voice to become higher in tone. Lower voices are known to be more attractive to listen to, more credible and more believable. You should be using your voice at its optimum pitch – find this out by using the exercise later in this chapter. Finding your optimum pitch, practising it and working with it often helps you to avoid getting higher and higher in your pitch.

Kriss Akabusi is a master at changes of tone and volume in his presentations. One minute he will have the audience hyped up with the excitement in the stadium at the Tokyo Olympics, and the next he will lower his tone completely to almost a whisper, to demonstrate the tension before the race – a powerful and effective tool.

Pauses and Non-silent Pauses

Pauses are powerful elements to add to presentations, as discussed in Chapter 7. However, do make sure they are silent pauses and not filled with 'um', 'er' and 'mm', which is irritating and distracting. Also avoid too much use of fillers like 'actually', 'basically', 'you know what I mean', 'like', 'right' and 'I mean'. Overuse of these can make your audience feel uncomfortable. I remember being in a meeting a while ago where one of the group proudly announced at the end that [John] had used the word 'basically' 46 times in the space of a 30-minute meeting. It was obviously so incredibly distracting that [Ben] had spent the entire meeting counting! Do watch repetition of words and phrases – it can label you as nervous and under-confident as well as detracting from your real message.

Good Voice Needs Good Posture

Walk tall, stand tall and sit tall – don't slump. Slumping will dampen the energy and vitality in the voice. It also affects how deeply you can breathe, and therefore the strength of the voice that comes out. Your feet are your anchor when giving a presentation – keep them parallel, and roughly hip-width apart, so that you're grounded and centred. Check that your head is centred – imagine a silk thread coming up out of your crown so that you're gently loosened upwards. Watch that you don't push your chin forwards too much, or tuck it in, as this creates neck strain and distorts your voice quality.

Voice Care

We tend to take our voice for granted and don't think about looking after it unless it is our living – for example, a singer. But for business people who communicate all the time with the voice – in meetings, on the telephone, at presentations – then it should be considered one of your major business tools and, like any tool, you should take care of it and know how to get the best from it. First, check you are using your voice where it is comfortable – each voice has its own natural or optimum pitch. Frequently pushing your voice up to compete with noise, or down to sound authoritative, may damage your voice – and then it is not easy to listen to. To find your optimum pitch, make a sound of agreement in a relaxed state – 'mm, mm'. The second sound should represent your optimum pitch. If you are speaking to a large audience, always make sure you check the need for amplification to avoid straining the voice. Avoid noisy and smoky clubs and bars the night before an important interview, meeting or presentation.

Trainers should rest their voice and try not to train regularly on consecutive days. Introducing more group exercises into training sessions can help to rest the voice if continuous training is commonplace. Some actors have 'rest days' where they don't use their voice at all for a whole day.

Look after your voice by drinking plenty of still water – up to 2 litres a day. Regular speakers should start drinking first thing in the morning as it takes a while to get round the body and to the voice. Frequent throat clearing can be harmful, sounds grating and is irritating, so try to swallow or take a sip of water instead. Avoid drinking caffeine or alcohol before a presentation – this will dry the throat. If the mouth becomes dry in a presentation, try licking the teeth or gently pressing your tongue on the roof of your mouth – both will produce more saliva. Lemon and honey or hot water can be good too.

Telephone Voice

A good proportion of your working week will be spent on the telephone, so it is a good idea to give some consideration to your telephone voice. Your 'voice image' is pretty important when it is the only medium through which people can judge you. In fact, on the telephone the impact you make with your voice rises to 84 per cent of the overall impression, from 38 per cent face to face.

To feel more in control and to help your voice to sound more powerful, you can stand up while on the phone. You have to *feel* assertive to *be* assertive, and standing up makes you feel more in control than in a relaxed sitting position. Smiling on the phone can help you to sound more friendly and approachable, bringing a pleasant tone to the voice – try it, it works! Using the other person's name has impact too, especially to get attention at the beginning – try starting your conversation or message off with 'Peter, Good Morning', instead of 'Good Morning Peter'. Use the name intermittently throughout the conversation too, although if you overdo it, this will have the opposite effect.

Accents are often a great asset on the telephone, as long the words are clear and well articulated. Many call centres are now based in the North of England for the very reason that accents are attractive and are therefore conducive to effective customer service and successful selling.

However busy and stressed you are, don't spoil your 'voice image' by showing this in your tone. Always answer and speak in a warm and relaxed manner and don't rush to say your name and/or company. Take a breath first before picking up the phone. In an age of email communication, remember that a phone call often has much more impact than an impersonal email message.

Answerphone and Voicemail Messages

We all have these nowadays and they can be incredibly irritating, so at least make sure that your message reflects and reinforces the personal brand values that you would like it to. Keep it brief but make sure that your voice sounds approachable and friendly. You never know who might be ringing you, and you want them to call back. Always return calls – again, this makes a big difference in a world where basic courtesy seems to be diminishing. Avoid having messages on your answer machine that sound like you're in a fish tank and remember that tones of Freres Jacques went out with the big shoulder pads!

chapter 7

Added Impact Presentations

IN THIS AGE OF THE INTERNET, CONFER-
ence calls and video conferencing, the 'people
element' of any business is becoming more and
more important in terms of communication, as
well as continuing to be an influential and powerful differentiator for organizations. People buy
from people, not from companies. Senior managers and directors increasingly realize that in
order to run their companies effectively and successfully, they need to get out of their offices and
communicate directly with their staff and
clients, and get in front of audiences and on TV
screens. Even those of you who are not in senior
management positions will be finding that greater
personal exposure is needed in order to move
where you want to in your career. So we have to
make sure that we make good use of our personal

image as a fundamental and powerful business tool and increase our face-to-face communication wherever possible. There is nothing as visually persuasive as ourselves, and therefore by understanding the key pointers to achieving a positive personal impact provided in this book, you will create and maintain a powerful and consistent differentiator over others.

This chapter focuses on what is probably the greatest opportunity for influencing and making a positive impact in business – that of audience presentations. However, unfortunately presentations also provide wide scope for a convincing loss of credibility faster than you can imagine! Often has it been known for a smart and capable businessman or woman to crumble under the pressure of public speaking. Thomas Leech once said, 'Brilliance without the capability to deliver it is worth little in any enterprise' (Leech, 1993). Such true words – a huge number of business professionals dent their hard-earned image when addressing an audience. I have met and worked with many business people over the years who assume that because they know their subject inside out and they know how to move their mouth and speak, they can therefore make effective presentations. Certainly, knowing your subject is essential, and this will give you confidence to stand up and talk about it: however, this alone is a far cry from presenting your message in a way that is clearly understood and acted on. In his book *Presenting to Win* Khalid Aziz defines a successful business presentation as: 'One which modifies the behaviour of the audience so that they do something in your favour that they would not have done had you not spoken to them' (Aziz, 2001). So, getting your message across alone does not define a successful presentation, unless your audience are inspired to do something with it too. Three fundamental points to remember for making effective presentations are:

- Be individual and unique
- Keep their attention
- Give them memorable messages and inspiration for taking action.

The aim in this chapter is not to reinvent the wheel but rather to bring your attention to and highlight the areas in which you can make real impact, and perhaps more so to help you to avoid and overcome the most common mistakes people make when speaking to audiences. This material has been gleaned from years of presenting to audiences and from a vast amount of putting into practice various bits of advice from reading and feedback from respected colleagues and friends. Believe me, being only 5′ 2″, I have had to use all the help I can get to become an effective presenter! So, I hope this knowledge will help you to perfect your presentations, become a major differentiator for your business, earn you added credibility and propel you forward towards greater exposure and financial success in your career.

Be Yourself

The first thing I want to point out is the importance of being yourself when presenting. Think back to Chapter 2, when we talked about being individual and it being one of your biggest assets. A notable number of the presentations I have listened to over the years have been either scripted or spoken in a way that is totally different from the speaker's true personality. This is obvious from the apparent discomfort they are experiencing by standing up and talking. If you observe the difference between an average business presentation and an experienced international speaker, you will instantly notice the personality of the speaker coming through via the body language and voice and the conversational language used by the experienced speaker. They are *being themselves*, and building a rapport with the audience immediately because their language is understood and spoken from the heart. The world's best communicators, such as Ex-President Bill Clinton and Prime Minister Tony Blair, have become known as such due to their conversational techniques in the way they present to an audience. Even though many of their speeches will have been written for them, they have been written in *their* language and in *their* personal style. Most competent business professionals can get their message across with the desired impact in an internal meeting where they feel comfortable and relaxed, but put these same people in front of an audience of 500 + people and the likelihood is that they fail to use this valuable opportunity to influence others to maximum effect. In fact, it is true to say that a large number create a negative impact and leave the audience feeling confused about their abilities. Much of this is due to the way they appear to change their *personality* to speak. In order to be yourself when you speak to audiences, you first need to be *confident* with yourself and your image. The other chapters in this book have helped you along this road, so you already have the inner confidence in yourself to be individual and communicate naturally. I will always remember a course I took many years ago called Effective Business Writing. When attempting to compile a letter outlining benefits to a potential client to secure a meeting, I was struggling with finding the right words. The instructor said to me, 'what is it you actually want to say'? I replied in my conversational tone what it was I wanted to convey and the answer back was 'then write that'. I often find myself remembering those simple yet wise words when preparing a presentation now. So, my message here is clear – do not change your personality to address an audience, keep your language conversational and be yourself.

The Spoken Word v The Written Word

Far too many business people still believe that the best way to convey a new initiative or new way of doing things in the company is by writing to all employees, or through a written press release to get the information out to their clients and potential clients. If they only stopped to assess their own reading habits and how they quickly scan information and absorb little, or the amount of information that does not get read at all, they may realize just how much impact they are losing by not making the effort to get face to face with people. I have seen this with dress code memos, as I mentioned in Chapter 4 – they not only lack impact but also create a confusion potentially detrimental to corporate image. It is far better to convey such important messages in person with the spoken word. We have the ability to *punctuate* and *accentuate* where we want to, without the risk of the listener interpreting the message incorrectly. We can even repeat a message two or three times to ensure it gets across, whereas we cannot guarantee that the reader will return to an important area and remember it. We also have the added advantage of *seeing* our audience and being able to interpret their reactions and adjusting our method of delivery accordingly. We can add pauses to emphasize and ensure that a particular point is absorbed and visualized, therefore stored and remembered. In other words, you have a control over the communication you have with your audience that you do not have with your reader. So, it is safe to say, then, that presentations are a great opportunity to influence and get your message across with the desired impact, but the fact is that a vast number of business professionals who are brilliant at their jobs completely waste an ideal opportunity to influence a captive audience with their ideas and beliefs – the lack of a good delivery system is one of the biggest skill deficiencies for business professionals today.

Walking Tall in Your Presentations

So, how do you take your presentation skills and improve on them for greater impact? I want to reiterate the point about *being yourself* and then ask you to work on the following areas. First, though, I need you to think about how *you think you come across* to an audience. Write down some words that you think describe you when you present. Some examples might be:

- Confident
- Natural
- Passionate
- Enthusiastic
- Natural body language
- Engage the audience
- Interesting
- Humorous
- Clear voice
- Enjoying yourself
- Looking the part

- Obviously nervous
- Uncomfortable
- Boring
- Monotone voice
- Irritating gestures
- Speaking too fast
- No pauses
- Rely on visual aids
- Rely on a script
- Rushing to finish

The next step is to get feedback. Video your next presentation and ask a respected colleague to sit in and give you feedback too. By using both methods and using the chart below, you will receive valuable and comprehensive feedback on your strengths and weaknesses. You should ask your colleague to be candid and direct with their feedback. A word of warning: never record and watch yourself on video just before an important presentation – you could run the risk of knocking your confidence completely and destroying your chances of making a positive impact. You will not have time to work on correcting elements that you have picked up on: if you are using video feedback, always make sure you do it a few weeks in advance to give you time to work on your irritating habits or other distractions.

Do this exercise for yourself when reviewing a video of your presentation, and get feedback from others too.

1 = not at all
5 = very

Opening

a) High impact		1 2 3 4 5
b) Confident		1 2 3 4 5
c) Effective		1 2 3 4 5
d) Created interest		1 2 3 4 5

Voice

a) Easy to hear		1 2 3 4 5
b) Easy to understand		1 2 3 4 5
c) Well paced		1 2 3 4 5
d) Good use of pauses		1 2 3 4 5
e) Good modulation and tone		1 2 3 4 5
f) Articulate		1 2 3 4 5
g) Language appropriate for the audience		1 2 3 4 5
h) Phrase repetitions		1 2 3 4 5

Body Language

a) Effective		1 2 3 4 5
b) Appropriate		1 2 3 4 5
c) Distracting		1 2 3 4 5
d) Eye contact with entire audience		1 2 3 4 5

e) Takes control of the room   1 2 3 4 5

f) Appears relaxed   1 2 3 4 5

Rapport

a) Includes passion and enthusiasm   1 2 3 4 5

b) Includes emotion   1 2 3 4 5

c) Likeable   1 2 3 4 5

d) Deals with audience response well   1 2 3 4 5

e) Material and delivery tailored to audience   1 2 3 4 5

f) Good use of stories   1 2 3 4 5

g) Inappropriate humour   1 2 3 4 5

h) Held audience attention   1 2 3 4 5

Purpose

a) Clear messages   1 2 3 4 5

b) No more than three clear points   1 2 3 4 5

c) Addressed the needs of the audience   1 2 3 4 5

d) Inspired audience to take action   1 2 3 4 5

e) Memorable messages   1 2 3 4 5

f) Good flow to presentation   1 2 3 4 5

Visual Aids

a) Good quality   1 2 3 4 5

b) Distracting   1 2 3 4 5

c) Easy to understand   1 2 3 4 5

d) Were an aid to the presentation   1 2 3 4 5

e) Effective use of   1 2 3 4 5

Ending

a) Strong message to close   1 2 3 4 5

b) Finished on time   1 2 3 4 5

c) Called for action   1 2 3 4 5

The Basics

All too often, the basics can be forgotten when you are focused on getting your message across. Your presentation should be built on two elements: what you want to *say* and what your audience wants to *hear*. Often these two factors are miles apart, but you need to find the common ground in order to make the impact you need. An audience always wants to know up front what is in it for them, what the benefits are to them and what they arc going to be able to do or understand better as a result of your talk. So find that common ground before you start planning. Unless they hear the benefits to them, your audience will switch off very quickly.

Your audience are the most important part of your presentation, and you need to tailor your material to suit. This is a common problem for speakers – if your delivery is not appropriate, then you will have wasted your time, or, worse still, damaged your image, reputation and professionalism. You may have a similar message to impart to two different audiences. For example, your presentation is about the need to introduce some new computer software to your company. Your presentation to the board would need to include messages of:

- Cost effectiveness
- Increased customer service
- Improved efficiency
- Possible savings due to a reduction in workforce.

When presenting the new idea to the rest of the employees, your message will be the same but a different delivery will be needed to make a positive impact. Your approach may include messages of:

- A move forward with the right technology
- Making their life easier and helping them to become more efficient
- More time for creative work.

You can see that by using the same delivery system to each audience you could easily alienate them within the first few minutes if you don't understand where they are coming from and recognize their needs and the potential benefits to them specifically. Make sure that you know your audience, plan well and deliver accordingly.

Begin Strong

Your opening is your best opportunity to make a powerful impact and to ensure that everybody in the room listens from the time you stand up, so make it good and don't waste the chance. Use a humorous anecdote, not necessarily a joke, or a quote or something to grab attention, but know your audience and what will work for them and their industry, role, culture and needs. Avoid the temptation to say 'it is an honour to be asked here today . . . ' or 'thank you for inviting me to speak to you on the subject of . . . ', or profuse apologies for something. This is pretty much guaranteed to turn off your listeners because they will assume that the rest of the presentation will be delivered in the same uninspiring and uncreative manner. Instead use something to create reaction or emotion or even say something provocative. You will then have them engaged and wanting more. I sometimes use the line 'Image kills . . . doesn't it?', or even stand in silence for 15 seconds and then tell the audience that they have now judged how capable, professional, credible, confident and creative I am even before I open my mouth! So, give some thought to your opening lines – it will be time well spent. Remember, you never get a second chance to make that all-important first and lasting impression.

Prompts and Notes

There are various forms of prompts for presentations:

Slides or visual aids

Bullet points

. . . or completely ad-lib.

You notice that I have left out a full script as an option. This is because I firmly believe that a presentation becomes a 'speech' if it is read word for word. A written speech can be needed at certain times – for political situations, for example – but rarely does it carry any impact whatsoever in a business situation. If you have a full script you will be tempted to read word for word and it could confuse you if you are not able to scan in a large chunk of text and repeat. As mentioned earlier, conversational and natural talk is many times more effective than an unspontaneous reading, and enables you to engage the audience more fully. A written speech is unlikely to allow you to bring out your personality and will force you to reduce your eye contact with the audience to a very low and ineffective level.

Visual Aids

Your visual aids should never act as crutches for you – they should be there to emphasize key messages but not to lead your presentation. Although they can act as prompts, never be tempted to merely go through and reiterate the items on a slide, point by point, as this is tedious and unnecessary. Don't be led by your visual aids either – keep control of the flow yourself. Your visual aids are there to augment and enhance your presentation and not to take over. This is something we have to be careful of when software such as Microsoft PowerPoint is becoming so powerful in terms of imagery, gimmicky transitions, colours and sounds. If your slides are too flashy, they will take over and distract your audience away from you and your words. Remember, *you* are the important element of your presentation, not your equipment – *you* should be in the spotlight. When a slide has been shown, you may want to continue talking – use the 'b' key on your keyboard to blank out the screen and bring attention back to you rather than have people looking at the screen instead. You can use the 'b' key again to bring back the picture.

Bullet Points

Bullet points on cards are by far the best prompt for a professional and slick presentation. Single words are best to avoid you being distracted by reading an entire sentence, or, worse still, half a sentence that leaves you wondering in a moment of panic what you meant by that! Write your bullet points out on postcard-sized cards, linked together or numbered in case of a disaster on the floor. Write in pencil and in capital letters – this allows you to rub out if you need to instead of scribbling over with a pen, creating a tendency to be distracted by the crossed-out word. The capital letters are much more easily readable in an instant. No audience will remember everything you have said, so bullets of your key points will help you to make sure you cover these and will also keep you on track.

Ad-libbing

Complete ad-libbing, without prompts at all, should be avoided. Even the most professional of speakers has been known to 'dry up' and lose track. Having notes shows the audience that you have bothered to plan and think about the presentation. Written notes also allow you to pause more easily between points by giving you the opportunity to view the next point while pausing. It shows the audience that you are going on to the next point and gives them time to absorb the last message.

Key Points

Do not overdo the number of key points you make in a presentation. As you know, there is a limit to how much information an audience will take away, so it is better to stick to a maximum of three and reiterate these as you go through. Too much information and each point becomes absorbed into the other.

Remember the theory:

- Tell them what you're going to tell them
- Then tell them
- Then tell them what you've told them.

If you can get your key points across with the impact and action you need then your presentation has succeeded.

Do not over-rehearse, which may not be advice that you're used to hearing. Over-rehearsing takes the spontaneity out of your presentation. It can make you over-confident and then cause you to panic if you forget your well-rehearsed thread, rather than being spontaneous and natural in your delivery.

Endings

Your ending is just as important as your beginning – this is your parting shot and you need to leave the audience with a positive message and something to think about. Your ending should include:

- A summary of your key points
- An action for your audience
- Inspiration for your audience to do something different.

Anecdotes and emotional stories also make good endings and leave your audience with a vivid memory of your presentation.

Speaking too Fast? – Pause for Thought

Many people feel that they talk too fast in presentations, and, yes, it can be a natural tendency when our adrenalin is increased and an element of nerves exists. Our brain processes words at a rate of about 500 words a minute, but our mouth can only speak them at an average of 130 words a minute. When we're speaking, our brain is already on to the next bit. You could describe this in terms of computer software and hardware – the computer software can process thousands of instructions a second, but the hardware, the printer, can print at only a fraction of the rate: hence we sometimes overload the system when the buffer to the printer gets full and basically tells us to stop processing new information until it catches up. So, could we be in danger of confusing our audience? When we learn that the human brain is capable of absorbing up to 180 words a minute over a long period of time it is clear that speaking too fast is not necessarily a problem. However, to ensure that our audience have grasped our message, created a picture and absorbed it, we need to create pauses regularly. Your audience cannot think about the last message when you are talking about the next. A pause also allows time for our output device (mouth) to catch up with our software (brain) and restructure our next collection of words. Think of this scenario as a glass of champagne being poured – if you pour it too quickly, it bubbles over and fails to become stored in the glass. However, if it is poured more slowly with pauses in between, more is stored in the glass without being wasted. In your next presentation, try to add in pauses at key points for as long as you can – they will always seem longer to you than to the audience. These 'breaks' will allow everybody in your audience to register and remember your key messages.

Creating Pictures

As I mentioned at the start of the book, we live in a visual world – a world where we believe what we *see* rather than what we *hear*. In fact, 95 per cent of the information that the brain takes in is through the eyes and only 5 per cent is from touch, taste, smell and sound. So, if we can create pictures in our mind, then we retain information more readily. It makes sense then to make use of pictures in your presentations, either by use of visual aids or by creating them in the mind of the listener. In fact, the picture I created in your mind just now with the champagne being poured will probably be one of the things you remember from this book when next making a presentation. So use this very powerful technique to make real impact and leave your audiences with vivid pictures and visual reminders of your key messages. I know people who have come up to me months later and mentioned some of the stories I have told them, and who tell me one in return. Using props can also create powerful images to help your key points to be memorable. For example, I have seen presenters use boxing gloves to demonstrate fierce competition or a video of baby animals with their mothers to demonstrate that we all need support to be successful.

Dress and Grooming

Your clothes and grooming will never be on show more than when you are in front of an audience. Any distractions will, without doubt, be picked up on. Some presentation skills books fail to attach an appropriate level of importance to the way we present ourselves visually, and to how vital this is in getting our message across. This is potentially misleading and dangerous – those people who cannot be bothered to pay attention to their dress and grooming will latch on to this with disastrous consequences. You have only got to apply common sense and real-life experiences to this theory to recognize that the way we dress is vital in getting across our desired messages of quality, credibility and respect for our audience. Your audience will appreciate your attention to your personal presentation and you will earn deserved respect and trust. Never forget that your personal packaging, as covered in detail in Chapter 3, is vital to creating personal power and impact. When you're presenting you will be under intense scrutiny, so attention to detail with dress and grooming is essential so as not to create distractions. When we're talking about confidence being key to being yourself in a presentation, then looking good and feeling good about the way you look are essential factors to a successful performance.

Key Dress Tips

- Always wear a jacket – you may not earn the respect and credibility you deserve without it.
- Choose fabrics in suits and jackets that do not crease easily and always press your clothes beforehand.
- Your clothes must fit well, with trousers and sleeves the correct length.
- Avoid anything that may cause a distraction – for example, elaborate jewellery, tie too short, scuffed shoes and so on.
- Avoid wearing glasses if you can – this weakens your eye contact.
- Women should avoid flat shoes – they look too casual when presenting on a stage.
- Wear clothes that are suitable for a lapel microphone to be attached to. Dresses do not work.
- Dress appropriately for your audience and the environment.

Make-up

If you are under strong lights on a stage, then you need to make sure that you don't look washed out. Follow these key tips:

- Foundation make-up is essential for men and women, with some blusher on the cheeks for women to add colour.
- There can be a tendency to wear more make-up on a stage, but keep it modest to avoid any one feature standing out too much.
- Avoid very strong coloured lipsticks which can make you look all lips.
- Blue and green eye shadows stand out more and can make you look severe.
- Sparkling eye shadows can be distracting because they catch the light.
- Too much eyeliner can give you the appearance of circles under the eyes.

Your 'Backside'

When considering your clothes, do remember to pay attention to your 'backside' too. In presentations you will inevitably turn your back from time to time and expose potentially your sloppiest angle. Keep your jackets crease-free and don't wear them to travel in. Check for any stray pet hairs and dandruff. Men must get rid of any excess neck hair that looks unkempt, and make sure your tie is properly tucked under your collar. And don't forget the backs of shoes and heels too.

Enthusiasm and Passion

The best presentations are delivered by people who have an absolute passion for their subject, which is displayed in the enthusiastic approach they adopt when they address an audience. Listeners respond better to a talk with passion rather than to a 'speech'. I have personally learned in my job as an image expert that people like to know that I am human too and that, yes, I do make mistakes occasionally, but I learn from them and make sure that they don't happen again. So, my presentation techniques are very much based on the passion I have for my job and my enthusiasm to pass on tips and knowledge that will help others in their professional careers. My audiences value this and, I am told, go away feeling inspired and enthused to make changes and improvements for themselves. Why should your audience be excited or enthusiastic if you aren't? I shall always remember my very first presentation to a bunch of executives in local government. I was so intent on using the right words and using gestures, as I had been taught to do and as I had rehearsed over and over, that, when talking about a 'narrow track', for some unknown reason I proceeded to open my arms wide to my sides creating a completely inconsistent gesture! If only I had known then that by being myself and being enthusiastic I could have been far more effective and not so hung up on using all the gestures I had been taught to use.

Voice Quality

From earlier in the book we know that our voice quality represents a significant percentage of the impact we make when we communicate on the phone, face to face or to an audience. I have included here some voice specifics when presenting.

- Warm up your voice before you start a presentation. If you don't do this, your voice could start off weak and croaky. Try facial exercises as described in Chapter 6 and make a phone call, sing in the car or do anything to get the vocal cords moving.

- Clarity – accents are no longer considered a hindrance to communication as long as your speech is articulate and clearly understood. In fact, most people enjoy listening to different accents if no effort is required to understand them.

- Modulation – if you tend to speak in one tone or at one level of volume, then you need to work on this. You will send your audience into a sleepy trance and miss your chance to make an impact.

- Pace – we all tend to speak faster when we do a presentation for real than in rehearsals. Try to vary your pace and slow down for key points and pause afterwards.

Eye Contact

Good use of eyes can really enhance your presentation. Those present-ers who consistently read notes and limit their audience eye contact really miss out on a great opportunity to draw in and engage everybody in the room. My key eye contact tips are:

- Vary your eye contact around the room, making everybody in the room feel involved in your presentation. Do not move your eyes around too quickly or you will look nervous and create the opposite effect. Rest your eyes for about 4–5 seconds in one part of the audience. You don't want to be conscious of this as you are speaking, so it is important to practise so that you feel comfortable with it.

- Avoid continually being drawn to that nice, smiley, friendly face in the front row who keeps nodding!

- Use eye contact when you have made a key point, and pause – very powerful.

- Never avoid eye contact when making a point – it will be lost.

- You need to ensure that everybody in the room feels that you are talking to them – eye contact is a great way of achieving this.

- Eye contact should not be a mechanical scanning process – use it to 'talk' to each person.

- Use your eyes to convey a smile – it looks more sincere.

Smiling is an important part of your presentation – for people to buy into your message, they need to like you too. Smiling can be difficult when the adrenalin is pumping and the nerves have really kicked in. I always carry a photograph in my briefcase of something that makes me smile, and I take a quick look at this before going on stage. My latest one is of my son with his wonderful smile, having fantastic fun on a sunny day in Animal Kingdom in Walt Disney World, Florida.

Jargon

You know you should avoid the use of jargon, but it is something that we tend to lapse into using without being conscious of it. It takes only one person in an audience not to understand a jargon word or phrase for it to be labelled as such. I experienced a classic example of the inappropriate use of business jargon at a conference for business-women last year. There was a series of breakaway sessions that delegates could attend and I decided to go along to one by a group of solicitors, because it was intended to be a case study of an area of business that I was particularly interested in at the time. In the first two minutes, confusing legal jargon had been used at least six times, and this continued to get worse until, after 5 minutes, I had completely switched off because I had lost track totally of the background to the case study and its purpose. Language that was common every day to these lawyers was completely alien to me and most of the audience.

The No-no's of Presenting

Although I do advocate and reiterate the importance of being you and being individual in your approach, there are certain elements that will be a complete distraction to your key messages and that should be avoided at all costs. Here are my top personal image wreckers for presentations:

- Hands in pockets constantly, jiggling with loose change or keys. Remove all bits and pieces from pockets beforehand. I have videoed people for coaching sessions and they've had no idea they were doing this! Avoid hands in and out of pockets generally.
- Lack of a jacket in a formal setting.
- Rolled-up shirt sleeves above the elbow.
- Unpolished and ill-maintained shoes – always visible when standing up in front of people.
- Constantly turning your back and talking to the flipchart or screen. The voice will be lost.
- Talking down to notes or the floor.
- Constant small and irritating gestures.
- Crossed legs when standing – always keep the feet slightly apart and maintain balance.
- Mumbling.
- Too much fact and not enough passion or emotion.
- Inappropriate clothing or bad grooming.

Pre Presentation Checklist

In the busy lives that we all lead, it is vital to have a checklist to refer to before a presentation, to avoid the obvious disasters. This is mine but you can add your own specifics to it:

To check:

- Room layout and size.

- Lighting.

- Projector equipment, if needed. Taking your own is usually safer.

- Other equipment needed in the room, including new flipchart pad.

- Microphone available if required – lapel mics are best.

- Final number of delegates for handouts and so on.

- Who is in the audience – be aware of influential people.

- Directions to venue. Check your route and approximate time to get there.

- Confirm start time and the time you need to arrive for set-up.

- Appropriate outfit – does it need to go to the dry-cleaners or need a repair?

- Have I clearly understood the brief for the session and the objectives?

Immediately beforehand and to take:

- Extension lead.

- All power cables and adaptors needed.

- Props and materials.

- Laptop.

- Your own flipchart pens.

- Backup of slides on CD.

- Polish shoes.

- Check yourself in full-length mirror.

- Shoes to drive in.

- Presentation notes.

- Emergency grooming kit.

Summary for Adding Impact to Your Presentations

- Plan every time and use a checklist.

- Find an overlap between what you want to say and what the audience wants to hear.

- Do not over-rehearse.

- Use passion, enthusiasm, fun and emotion.

- Use eye contact for effect and to engage the whole audience.

- Vary tone and modulation of the voice for interest.

- Pause regularly.

- Do not let your visual aids become crutches or overpower you.

- Do not include more than three key points.

- Create pictures and use stories.

- Use impactful beginnings and endings.

- Get feedback on all aspects of your presentation, using video.

- Be yourself and bring out your personality.

chapter 8

Interviews and Meetings

AN INTERVIEW IS CERTAINLY A TIME WHEN you will be wanting to make your biggest impact – a time when first impressions are vital to the next stage in your career. One-to-one meetings or those with a group of people are opportunities for you to reinforce your personal brand values and make an impact. This chapter focuses on the ways in which you can make a positive and memorable difference in these two common situations, building on the elements already covered in the book. Media interviews are your chance to be exposed to millions and to get your message across, in terms of personality, opinion or corporate selling points. Although this book does not cover media interviews in depth, a further book is being developed on this important subject in its own right.

Preparation for Interviews

First, remember that it is not always the best-qualified candidates who get the jobs, it is those who best 'sell' themselves to the interviewer. If you know you can do a job, then you should be able to 'sell' yourself in a way that gets you that job. For interviews, positive first impressions are more crucial than ever. Get it wrong and you will not get a second chance. Although a great first impression will not guarantee success, a poor one will almost certainly guarantee that you will not get through to the next stage. Preparation therefore is time well spent – in terms of researching the company and the role of course, and also in terms of how you present yourself. Remember that nothing is as visually persuasive as yourself, not even slick words, so spend an appropriate amount of preparation time on *you* too. Why take the trouble to produce a great CV and then not follow it through with positive *personal* impact? Remember how we said that 'great words will not erase a poor appearance'? In an interview, the interviewer will already have formed an expectation of you from your CV and possibly telephone conversations and emails. Make sure that your visual impact is consistent and as impressive. According to research with senior directors of Fortune 1000 companies, the quality of communication, both verbal and non-verbal, rather than qualifications, are key differentiators to their businesses. The sheer fact that you have an interview means that they believe you can do the job; now all you have to do is convince them that you are *the* best candidate for the job and right for their company.

If you don't know somebody who already works at the company interviewing you, visit the office beforehand and get a feel for the culture. Visiting around lunchtime when there is more activity through the front door and the reception area is a good idea. Look at the way people are dressed, are they friendly and smiley; are they dynamic in the way they move; can you recognize the management from the rest of the staff? You can glean a lot of information about a company's culture from observing in this way, and therefore you can work out how you can fit in and influence in this environment. Of course, you may also decide that this company is not for you for whatever reason. When you are in the interview hot seat, your interviewer will be assessing whether you will fit in and whether you successfully portray the corporate image, as well as whether you can do the job. They will be searching for something they can relate to and something they like about you. Generally people look for something they can personally connect with when communicating with others. Jo Bond, Managing Director of Right Management Consultants (Outplacement Consultants), says,

> With our candidates we encourage them to think about the organization's culture and branding, not just in regard to their products but their 'employee brand'. Looking at the company's website, corporate literature and, ideally, by visiting their offices in advance of their interviews, our candidates can research what is the best way to dress and present themselves so that they look as though they are already one of the 'in-crowd'.

What Do I Wear?

Dressing the part is important – you need to *look* like the sort of person they want to employ and like the sort of person who values their career. If you do not have a suitable outfit, then allow time before your interview, if possible, to find one. Remember that it may need altering to fit well and this can take a few days. The key thing is to look and feel comfortable in your outfit, and not restricted in any way.

For women, I recommend that you think carefully about whether a skirt suit is more appropriate than a trouser suit. On most occasions a trouser suit will be perfect, but some of the more traditional companies, particularly in finance and banking, may expect to see a woman in a skirt suit instead. Again a little bit of surveillance from the reception area can help with this in advance.

You may be told that the dress code is smart/casual or that it is dress-down Friday, but my advice is to play safe, remember that you need to make a positive *first* impression and dress in an appropriate suit, that you feel great in, with a tie for men. So that you don't appear stuffy, always make sure your suits are current, bring out personality with colour and patterns in ties or tops, and finish off with well-chosen accessories. Occasionally you may be *asked* to come smart/casual – this sometimes happens on the second or third interview, where you may also be asked to provide a presentation. If this is the case, then adhere to the rules provided in Chapter 4, and dress towards the top end of the business casual scale. Remember that darker colours will have more impact, but avoid solid black, as it can be intimidating.

Grooming

Research shows that more than three-quarters of professional people believe that the way their colleagues are groomed has a direct effect on how professional they are perceived to be and therefore on how well they do their jobs. Your grooming is therefore a key area to attend to for interviews. You *will* be scrutinized and any distractions can add up to a negative first impression. In fact, David Goldstone, Director of Osprey Clarke Executive Search, told me that: 'I literally scrutinize a candidate's image on interviewing and make notes accordingly. Personal presentation is such an important indication of a person's values and respect for others that I feel totally justified in making it a part of the recruitment process'. Recent research also shows that people who wear perfumes and aftershaves to interviews are less likely to get the job. Overpowering fragrances can be offensive, so keep them to a subtle body freshener or perhaps fresh, citrus-based men's products. Do adhere to the grooming guidelines in Chapter 3 and make a note that the following points are in particular known to be interview disasters:

Interview Grooming Gaffes

- Bad breath
- Smoking odour on clothes/breath
- Overpowering fragrance
- Unfresh clothes
- Unclean hair
- Badly bitten or dirty nails
- Dandruff on shoulders – easily visible on dark suits
- Ill-fitting clothes – you'll look as though they have been borrowed for the occasion!
- Snagged tights
- Clothes that are past their best or that are dated

On Arrival

Arriving on time is pretty obvious, but do make the necessary checks on journey time beforehand. Never arrive looking flustered, stressed or harassed, even if you are. This is majorly off-putting to your interviewer and suggests nervousness and a lack of confidence. Allow time to visit the cloakroom when you arrive and check yourself in a full-length mirror if there is one. Check teeth for bits in between and use a breath freshener. Women, check for lipstick on the teeth too. If the nerves have kicked in, then do some deep breathing to help release the tension and relax you a little.

Make sure you keep your right hand free for handshakes – just carry one item, either briefcase or leather folder, and avoid carrying newspapers and gadgets separately. If you are being met from a reception area, be aware that you may be observed by reception staff too – be friendly and confident and avoid any aggressive language or behaviour, to them or while on the phone to other people. It is best to switch off the mobile phone before you arrive in the building.

When working with outplacement and recruitment companies, I am frequently asked, 'Do I offer a handshake in an interview?' Unless you are faced with a panel of people, when a handshake with each would be inappropriate, I always advise that you offer a handshake. If you don't, you could be in danger of appearing under-confident and unprofessional. It is your chance to make an immediate impression, with firm handshake (make sure you have had feedback on it, though, as in Chapter 5), good eye contact and a smile.

Wait to be offered a seat, sit comfortably and confidently and avoid crossing your arms. For women, if you are wearing a short-length skirt, just cross the legs comfortably at the ankle or keep both feet on the floor.

Remember the mirroring discussed in Chapter 5 – for example, do not lean forward with elbows on the table if your interviewer is sitting in a more relaxed position, leaning back in the chair. Interviews held across a table create a barrier to communication and present a superiority situation for the interviewer. If you have a choice of seating, avoid this situation and instead opt for sitting at a table at a 90° angle to your interviewer or sitting without a table at all. As an interviewer, consider how formal or informal you want the interview to be and arrange the seating accordingly. Round tables are a good choice and generally applicants will be more themselves if they are in a more relaxed atmosphere. If you are offered refreshments, consider whether you will be comfortable drinking coffee or whether water would be best. Caffeine can dry the mouth.

The Interview

So, you have made your positive first impression, and you now need to make an impact in the way you manage the interview. An interview is a test of your total image and how well you project it. I am not about to go into heaps of detail about the interview process itself, but rather will provide you with pointers to add real impact. Interviews are artificial situations but their outcome is crucial to your career progression. First and foremost, be yourself – you will come across as much more sincere and credible if you do.

Take with you a quality pen and leather folder to take notes – both of these portray a professional image, attention to detail and high standards. A good-quality fabric folder will be acceptable too, but make sure it doesn't look shabby and is not filled with bits of paper from previous meetings. Always wear a watch – without one your time-management skills will be in question. Remember that the interview is a two-way process and you need to make sure that this company is right for you too, so take short notes when appropriate. Take a diary too in case there is a need to make a date to come back.

Sit upright and alert rather than slouching, and be aware of your posture. When listening, use relaxed gestures – for example, keep your hands visible on the table, or gently clasped or folded. Steady eye contact is important – it will show confidence and interest when listening. Avoid looking down at notes or out of the window when the interviewer is speaking, but do break eye contact occasionally so as not to appear intimidating or to be hanging on to every word the interviewer says. When answering challenging questions like 'so tell me why you've had three jobs in two years', retain good eye contact and don't fiddle so as not to appear insecure. Don't cross arms or legs in this situation, as it will appear defensive. Just be relaxed and answer confidently – these are questions you need to have prepared well for.

Avoid excessive laughter in interviews. A sense of humour and smiling is important, but over-use of laughter will render you nervous and you may not be taken seriously. Enthusiasm, however, plays a big part in selling yourself – interviewers are influenced by this and consider it a vital qualification for any job.

Delegates in senior roles in my seminars at outplacement companies occasionally raise the question of how assertive they should be in interviews. They know they are going for a senior leadership role but feel a little uncomfortable with how to and to what level to exude these skills at interview. Initiating the handshake will be your first assertive and confident gesture. You should take care to listen and not to interrupt at all. Use confident body language and good voice quality rather than relying on talking excessively to demonstrate presence and good leadership skills. The interviewer will certainly be looking for signs of a good manager and leader, but not an autocrat. Use the mirroring and language techniques as outlined in Chapter 5 and work on developing rapport and effective communication. Perhaps unfairly, interviewers tend to give jobs to people they like and know they can get on with.

Before leaving, be assertive: ask when you should expect to hear and what the next steps are. When leaving, again offer a handshake if it is not offered to you first, smile and thank the interviewer for his or her time.

Key 'Added Impact' Tips for Interviews

Prepare

- Find out sufficient information about the company.
- Observe the way people are dressed and the culture of the company, and plan accordingly.
- Anticipate difficult questions and prepare your answers.

Dress and Grooming

- Plan your clothes in advance to allow time for alterations and cleaning.

- Choose appropriate clothes for the industry and corporate culture.

- Avoid smart/casual dress unless specifically *asked* to dress this way.

- Immaculate grooming is essential:

  - Hair should be clean and long hair tied back – including men.

  - Don't wear overpowering fragrances.

  - Beards and moustaches can be offputting – consider whether you can do without them, at least for the interview.

  - Nails should be well manicured as they will be constantly visible.

  - Women should wear light yet professional make-up.

  - Cover any distracting blemishes with concealer.

- Dark, neutral colours for suits are best.

- Avoid loud and flashy ties.

- Make sure your shoes are polished.

- Use a quality leather folder and pen for taking short notes.

- Keep jewellery to a minimum.

- Look as professional as your well-written and presented CV.

Arrival

- Arrive on time and allow time for a visit to the cloakroom to take a last look at yourself in the mirror.

- Keep your nerves in check by using slow and deep breaths.

- Switch mobile phone off *before* arrival at the office.

- Be aware that you may be observed by reception staff too.

- Keep your right hand free for handshake.

- Do not appear harassed or flustered.

- Smile and be confident – they want to see you because you *can* do the job.

The Interview

- Retain good eye contact when listening.
- Do not interrupt.
- Do not use too much laughter, but smile!
- Look comfortable and appropriately relaxed.
- Do not be defensive when answering difficult questions.
- Do not fiddle – if you have a tendency to do this, keep your hands lightly clasped.
- Shake hands and thank the interviewer for their time when leaving.

A point for interviewers – an interview is a two-way process because you are also trying to 'sell' the idea of working for this company to the candidate. All too often, HR managers can present a staid, dated and conservative corporate identity through the way they dress. I am being asked more often than ever to work with local government organizations who are trying to attract and recruit younger people to join them. They know that until they succeed in revamping their out-of-date and 'stuck in the 1970s' image, they will not achieve this goal.

The Difference with Meetings

Meetings offer a regular opportunity to express yourself and to portray your ideas and professionalism to colleagues and managers. It is an opportunity to reinforce your credibility, creativity, communications skills, leadership ability and to earn respect and trust from others. Step back for a moment and reflect on how you think you come across at meetings. What would your colleagues say about you and how would they rate you in these areas? To create the right impact in meetings, the guidelines laid out for interviews above also apply. There are, however, a few points to add to ensure that you make the right impression and earn the respect you need.

Arriving on time is important in the UK. In some countries it is absolutely paramount and in others they take a more relaxed view. For example, in Latin American countries it is quite normal to arrive 15–20 minutes late for a meeting, whereas in South Africa punctuality is strictly observed. You are advised to check out specifics for different countries before travelling there. If you are late only apologize once instead of going into some long diatribe of what happened, unless it is particularly humorous. If arriving late for a meeting that has already started, avoid arriving looking flustered and 'falling' through the door loaded up with gadgets, briefcase, mobile phone, newspaper and so on. If you have a suitcase or suit carrier with you, always leave these in reception, rather than arrive at a meeting cluttered up. Make a bad entrance and your positive first impression is blown. Also, looking pleased to meet somebody is always a good start, but it is not always practised!

Group Meetings

Where there are several people in a meeting, vary your eye contact among everybody when talking, to keep their interest and involve them all – this is also empowering for you. Avoid directing your talk to just one or two people in the room. If you are able to have input into the layout of the room, then bear in mind that a long, narrow table will not allow you to have good eye contact with everybody. A horseshoe shape or round table is much better. Don't be afraid to get up and use the flipchart to illustrate a point or to add a welcome change of scene if you sense boredom. This all adds interest and clarity and brings the focus on you in a positive way. Be aware of other people's body language to ascertain how the meeting is going and how effective you are when speaking in getting your points across. You can use body language to indicate that you want to speak in a meeting rather than interrupting. For example, lean forward with your arms on the table, ready to speak. If you are asked to talk impromptu, take time to breathe and prepare your thoughts.

At the end of any meeting everybody should be clear about the next steps. If the plan of action is not clear, make sure that *you* suggest it is discussed and that somebody is minuting the actions clearly. Finally, if you have actions from a meeting, make sure you: a) set realistic time-scales and b) do what you say you are going to do in the agreed time-scales. In a busy office, it is incredibly irritating for people to have to chase you up and you will be labelled as unreliable and unprofessional, and your excuses of being 'too busy' will fall on deaf ears.

With regard to dress, remember that medium-depth, non-threatening shades are less formal and are more conducive to effective discussion in informal meetings, but being too casual can lose you authority in this situation. Be careful not to create barriers with your clothes for informal meetings by dressing as you would for a board meeting. A client of mine, a manager, described to me a situation when her boss's appearance was totally inappropriate for the meeting they had arranged. The meeting was to be over dinner between the two of them, therefore an informal setting outside of the office. It was a delicate subject and involved discussion about a member of staff. Even though these two people knew each other well, the discussion was hindered by the way the boss was dressed. He had chosen to wear, as he typically did every day in the office, his slick pinstripe suit and contrasting tie, whereas my client was dressed more appropriately in smart/casual clothes. The effect was that she felt very uncomfortable and not able to speak as freely as she would have done had he been dressed in a more relaxed way, even though she knew him well. The meeting was not a success. So, to reiterate: 'dress appropriately for the situation and environment'.

Key Tips for Making an Impact at Meetings

- Arrive on time.
- Do not arrive looking flustered or harassed.
- Get seated quickly.
- Do not fall through the door loaded up with gadgets, bags and newspaper under arm.
- Enter the room looking energetic and enthusiastic – this will rub off on the others and energize the group.
- Dress appropriately.
- Speak in the first few minutes.
- Show interest in others when they are speaking by using eye contact and positive body language.
- Take notes but not copious ones – it will look like you are taking minutes.
- Use body language to show you want to speak.
- Do not interrupt.
- Do not whisper to others while somebody else is speaking (although in France, for example, this can just mean that two people are talking about something that is not relevant to anybody else).
- Turn off your mobile, and wristwatches that beep on the hour.

Video Conferencing

This is an area of vast growth in business today, but I do not believe that it will or should ever replace face-to-face communication as the most effective business communication tool. Of course, there is a place for video conferencing where international business is extremely urgent or where it does not merit the time or cost of travel. It can be a daunting process for some people because of the camera, but you just need to talk as you would in a normal meeting. Keep your comments concise and to the point, in order not to let the meeting overrun – it is an expensive medium. If there is a monitor in the room that shows the picture as it appears at the other end, try not to be distracted by it but just use it to ensure that the correct person or visual is being shown.

Media Interviews

Whether a reporter has approached you or you have gone to them with a story, never is there a greater opportunity to present to such a large audience, potentially millions, your knowledge and expertise, your company's assets and your personal charisma. That is, of course, if you don't let your image get in the way. Be clear that you should use interaction with the media for your *own* benefit and to help *your* success. But also be aware that the media have a big role to play in either the success *or failure* of businesses. I have provided below my short, sharp tips for media interviews, but if this is to be a regular activity for you, you should seek advice from a media training company or read further about the skills needed.

- Preparation is key – never do an interview on a first discussion with a reporter, unless it is something you are used to commenting on and are prepared.
- Avoid the answer 'No comment' at all costs – never do a media interview unless you are prepared.
- Never get into a heated debate with the interviewer – you will almost certainly lose.

- Keep focused on your key points and repeat them – too much information and your key messages will be lost. Write down bullet points.

- Be clear about what you *do not* want to comment on and make sure the interviewer knows this.

- Do not talk too quickly and keep a good pace.

- Take note that the first things you say are the things most likely to be remembered.

For TV interviews:

- Dress appropriately and make sure there are no distractions. Avoid very bright colours and pure white (unless under a jacket) as these 'bleed' into the screen.

- Avoid 'busy' patterns as these strobe on the screen.

- Always wear make-up – men too. You will look washed out without it.

- Women, check for lipstick on the teeth.

- Check your appearance in the monitor before filming starts.

- Remember that your legs and feet may also be in shot.

- Always ask for a recording of the interview for your review.

Conclusion

A New Beginning . . .

HAVING NOW COMPLETED *WALKING TALL* you should have a clear idea of what needs to be done to create a powerful brand for yourself. The future starts *now*, when you embark on a continuous and exciting journey to self-discovery and image improvement. Do use all the things you've learned, not just from me but also from self-evaluation and feedback from others, to help you to create fantastic personal brand values, which will provide you with opportunities for greater exposure, success and financial reward. Remember, it is about being yourself but, most importantly, it is about being the best you can be. With all the guidance I hope I've provided you in this book, combined with your unique personal charisma and a positive mind, you should now have all you need to propel you towards major new beginnings with your image impact. I do hope you've enjoyed *Walking Tall* – I feel honoured that you have taken the time to read my book, and if you manage to feel even better about yourself and project yourself with more impact as a result, then I have achieved my goal.

Smile and be happy, and remember, when it comes to your image, reach for the moon, because if you miss you'll still be one of the stars!

If you have been inspired to take this subject further in your business and/or team, then we can help. For executive one-to-one coaching, or fun and motivating presentations, and workshops on image personal branding, please contact us at *www.leconsultants.co.uk*.

Further Reading and Useful Contacts

References

Aziz, Khalid (2001) *Presenting to Win*. Dublin: Oaktree Press.

Fink, Thomas, and Mao, Yong (1999) *The 85 Ways to Tie a Tie*. London: Fourth Estate.

Gobé, Marc (2001) *Emotional Branding – The New Paradigm for Connecting Brands to People*. New York: Allworth Press.

Leech, Thomas (1993) *How to Prepare, Stage and Deliver Winning Presentations*. New York: American Management Association.

Mehrabian, Albert (1971) *Silent Messages*. Belmont, CA: Wadsworth.

Olins, Wally (1991) *Corporate Identity*. London: Thames & Hudson.

Peters, Tom (1995) *In Search of Excellence*. London: HarperCollins Business.

Different Cultures and Etiquette

Elizabeth Urech (1997) *Speaking Globally*. London: Kogan Page.

Roger E. Axtell (1997) *Do's and Taboos Around the World*. New York: Wiley.

Voice

Cristina Stuart (2000) *Speak for Yourself*. London: Piatkus.

The Voice Care Network – 01926 864000

www.voicecare.org.uk

Body Language

Allan Pease (1997) *Body Language*. London: Sheldon Press.

Presentation Skills

Lee Bowman (1999) *High Impact Presentations*. London: Bene Factum Publishing.

Christian H. Godefroy and Stephanie Barrat (1998) *Confident Public Speaking*. London: Piatkus.

NLP (Neuro-Linguistic Programming)

Sue Knight (1997) *NLP At Work*. London: Nicholas Brearley.

Steve Andreas and Charles Faulkner (1998) *NLP – The New Technology of Achievement*. London: Nicholas Brearley.

Media Skills

Jerry Brown (1998) *Meet the Media with Your Agenda* (Tapes 1 and 2). USA: Author.

Clothes and Style

Kim Johnson Gross and Jeff Stone (1998) *Chic Simple Men's Wardrobe*. New York: Knopf.

Susie Faux (1998) *Susie Faux Wardrobe Solutions* (for women). London: New Holland.

Mary Spillane (1998) *The Makeover Manual*. London: Macmillan.

www.shirt-press.co.uk

www.thomaspink.co.uk

www.RichardAndersonLtd.com (bespoke tailor)

www.online-tailor.com (tailoring . . . 21st-century style)

www.extratall.co.uk

www.longtallsally.co.uk

www.box2.co.uk (for larger women)

Other

Alexander Technique Society of Teachers

020 7284 3338

www.stat.org.uk

Pilates

www.pilates.co.uk

www.flowpilates.com

Pierre Lang (UK) Jewellery

info@pierrelang4u.com

Color Me Beautiful (for individual colour and style consultations)

020 7627 5211

www.cmb.co.uk

Walking TALL Corporate Image Presentations and Workshops

www.leconsultants.co.uk

walkingtall@leconsultants.co.uk

Index

Other self-help books from McGraw-Hill

How to Get a Job You'll Love – A practical guide to unlocking your talents and finding your ideal career by LEES
Price: £14.99
ISBN: 0077098005

A unique and creative look at career planning. It takes one step back and teaches you how to think outside the box, tap into your hidden talents and identify what type of career you really want.

Living with Fear by MARKS
Price: £14.99
ISBN: 0077097580

Living with Fear is a self-help book that gives practical advice to people who are suffering from phobias, panic, obsessions, rituals or traumatic distress.

Manager's Guide to Self-Development by PEDLER et al
Price: £19.99
ISBN: 0077098307

This book is designed as a self-development programme for managers seeking to develop skills such as mental agility, creativity, social skills and emotional resilience.

Assertiveness at Work – A practical guide to handling awkward situations by BACK AND BACK
Price: £14.99
ISBN: 0077095332

Over 100,000 copies sold worldwide. This book is a practical guide for developing your own natural assertiveness to benefit both yourself and your organization.

Time Management 24/7 – How to double your effectiveness by PHILLIPS (forthcoming)
Price: £9.99
ISBN: 007709963X

Traditional time management techniques are no longer sufficient in our 24/7 economy. In offering advice on how to identify and focus on your priorities in life, change your behaviour and get the most out of electronic tools, this book shows you how to lead a more balanced life.

Fighting Back – Overcoming Bullying in the Workplace by GRAVES

Price: £9.99

ISBN: 0077099516

Fighting Back is a hard-hitting, authoritative guide to combating bullying in the work place. Taking a simple, straightforward approach , this book looks at how to recognise a bully, how to protect yourself, how to gather evidence, and the steps to take to make an immediate and lasting difference.

Open for Business – How to write letters that get results by FERGSUON

Price: £19.99

ISBN: 0077097696

The book aims to encourage readers to become more confident, effective writers. It looks at how to get started, how to overcome writer's block, how to write a five-minute outline, how to build up a rapport, how to promise and deliver benefits, and how to get a 'yes' result.

The Great Escape – Your guide to early retirement and financial freedom by WHITE

Price: £14.99

ISBN: 0077098412

The Great Escape is an accessible guide to planning early retirement.

Stepping Up – A woman's guide to career development by KAZEROUNIAN
Price: £19.99
ISBN: 0077098021

Based on interviews with women across Europe, this practical guide aims to help women overcome everyday challenges and develop their careers.

When Life Gives You Lemons: Remarkable Stories of People Overcoming Adversity by TRESNIOWSKI
Price: £12.99
ISBN: 007135591X

Rich in wisdom, hope, and intimate portraits of real people, this is a book which manages to capture the essence of courage, delivering a set of priceless lessons readers can immediately incorporate into their own lives. Alex Tresniowski relates 21 inspiring experiences of ordinary folks and then shows exactly how anyone can make the most of the vast stores of strength residing within us all.

Addicted To Unhappiness by HEINEMAN PIEPER
Price: £ 16.99
ISBN: 0071385495

The powerful new book by the bestselling author team of Martha and William Pieper, is based on the Piepers' discovery that the most common obstacle to fulfilment is a secret addiction to unhappiness.

How to Deal With Emotionally Explosive People by BERNSTEIN

Price: £ 10.99

ISBN: 007138569X

A valuable source of insight and guidance on how to deal effectively with the "walking time bombs" in our midst.

Why We Hate by DOZIER

Price: £ 18.99

ISBN: 0809224836

Why We Hate presents readers with a comprehensive nine-step strategy for controlling and eliminating hate.

Crucial Conversations- Tools for Talking When the Stakes Are High by PATTERSON

Price: £ 10.99

ISBN: 0071401946

Crucial Conversations offers readers a proven seven-point strategy for achieving their goals in all those emotionally, psychologically, or legally charged situations that can arise in their professional and personal lives.

Emotional Vampires: Dealing with People who Drain you Dry by ALBERT J. BERNSTEIN

Price: £ 9.99

ISBN: 0071381678

The best-selling author of Dinosaur Brains offers protection from people who seek to destroy the emotional and psychological well-being of others.

The Disease to Please – Curing the People-Pleasing Syndrome by BRAIKER
Price: £ 10.99
ISBN: 0071385649

The Disease to Please explodes the dangerous myth that 'people pleasing' is a benign problem. It is the first book to treat people pleasing as a serious psychological syndrome, and it breaks new ground in its approach to offer a cure.

If you wish to order any of the above books then please contact our Customer Services Department on Tel: + 44 (0) 1628 502700
Fax: + 44 (0) 1628 635895.